GARLAND STUDIES IN

Entrepreneurship

STUART BRUCHEY

Allan Nevins Professor Emeritus
American Economic History
Columbia University

GENERAL EDITOR

A Garland Series

Jacome's Department Store

Business and Culture in Tucson, Arizona, 1896–1980

June Webb-Vignery

Garland Publishing, Inc.

New York & London

1989

Library of Congress Cataloging-in-Publication Data

Webb-Vignery, June.
Jacome's Department Store : business and culture in Tucson, Arizona,
1896–1920 / June Webb-Vignery.
p. cm. — (Garland studies in entrepreneurship)
Includes bibliographical references.
ISBN 0-8240-3396-5 (alk. paper)
1. Jacome's Department Store—History. 2. Department stores—Arizona—
Tucson—History. 3. Mexican American business enterprises—Arizona—
Tucson—History.
I. Title. II. Series.
HF5465.U55T839 1989
381'.141'09791776—dc20   89-37800

Printed on acid-free, 250-year-life paper

Manufactured in the United States of America

ACKNOWLEDGMENTS

The idea of exploring Mexican-American culture and business management through the growth and development of Jacome's Department Store grew out of the perception that there was a lack of historical and management studies of Hispanic businesses. The Jacome family's donation of their papers to The University of Arizona in 1983 offered a splendid opportunity to pursue this subject in some detail. Using the Jacome papers, newspaper articles, and oral interviews with many of the "movers and shakers" of Tucson's business community during the days of Jacome's existence, I was able to develop a comprehensive historic account of the store's development and its interaction with the larger community.

Since this book traces the growth and disintegration of Tucson's downtown business district, which coincided with the rise and demise of Jacome's, I had the opportunity to interview many delightful and colorful native Tucsonans, including City Manager Joel D. Valdez, who first gave me an awareness and understanding of Tucson's Mexican-American community when I worked as a member of his staff at the City of Tucson. I also received some valuable insights from Maria Elba Molina, who first suggested the general topic of a Mexican-American entrepreneur. Yet, without the help of the Jacome family and other Tucson retailers, this project could not have been completed. I am sincerely indebted to Alex, Jr., Augustine, and Estela V. C. de Jacome not only for the access they provided to private papers, records, and photographs, but also for their willingness to share recollections of the store's development through numerous personal interviews. Their aid in contacting former employees, customers, and others who worked with the store was invaluable. A special thank you is also due to Tucson retailers Cele Peterson; Herb, Dave, and Ted Bloom; Jim Davis; Henry Quinto; and the late Leon Levy. Their interest and candid answers to questions provided a wealth of detail and a number of insights which documents alone could not have supplied.

The University of Arizona Special Collection's staff was also extremely helpful. Dr. Louis A. Hieb opened the uncatalogued Jacome collection, while Phyllis Ball provided other important sources and information. Equally generous was the staff of the Arizona Heritage Center and Dr. Harwood Hinton, who gave me helpful leads to research materials on Tucson's history.

i

An association of more than sixteen years with Professor Paul Carter of The University of Arizona had a profound effect on the development of this manuscript. His widely recognized talent for creative social and cultural inquiry is without equal. Also, Professor Richard Abrams of the University of California and Professor James Logan of The University of Arizona provided guidance on the central importance of business in American culture. To Professor Logan, I am especially indebted for introducing me to the ecology model of macro organizational behavior which equates an organization's survival with its ability to adapt to a shifting environment. This model is implicit in the text, and it provided an interesting way of viewing both Jacome's experience as compared to its Anglo competitors and the role of culture in organizational survival.

Finally, I would like to thank my parents, Roy and Thelma Webb, for helping me appreciate cultural diversity as well as giving me a basic understanding of the concepts of retailing through the family business. Most of all, however, I want to thank my husband, John Robert, for patiently reading the entire manuscript several times, making invaluable editorial suggestions, and for seldom grumbling even when awakened at 5:00 a.m. by the clacking of a typewriter. His love and support provided the impetus for completing the story of Jacome's Department Store.

TABLE OF CONTENTS

iii

CHAPTER ONE

THE BACKGROUND: CULTURE AND ENVIRONMENT

In 1896, Carlos C. Jacome and Loreto Carrillo opened "La Bonanza," a general mercantile shop in Tucson, Arizona.   Contributing three hundred dollars each to the enterprise, they rented a twelve-foot by thirty-five-foot room in an adobe building on Congress Street, the principal business thoroughfare of downtown Tucson.   "Drummers" guaranteed their credit and sold them merchandise to get started.   Crudely and meagerly furnished, their small shop was a typical "country store," with merchandise draped over every inch of the sales floor.   Some was even displayed on the planked sidewalk outside so those driving by in wagons and buggies might see it.[1]

From these meager beginnings evolved Jacome's Department Store, a fixture in downtown Tucson for eighty-six years.   Sole owner of the enterprise by 1913, Carlos brought the store to a prominent position in Tucson's business life, and his son, Alex, solidified that position. Prominent in the life of the community, both men also assumed leadership roles in Arizona.

As the store grew and prospered, it developed a distinctive image which set it apart from other retail establishments in the downtown business district.   An

1

important ingredient of this image was derived from the cultural background of its owners and managers. Of Hispanic origins, their culture played an important role in the store's development.

The interplay between culture and environment which characterized the development of Jacome's presents a valuable case study in Hispanic enterprise within the larger scope of American business. As one eminent Western historian has suggested, "The keepers of bodegas . . . the petite bourgeoisie in the Mexican-American barrios who have been the go-betweens between their own people and outside Anglos . . . takes on a larger cultural meaning which . . . we could explore with profit."[2] Multicultural in makeup and pluralistic in culture, the West has long had material available for historical studies of minority entrepreneurs. Mexican-American business offers an especially promising field of investigation.

The rapid increase of the Hispanic population in the United States suggests the need to explore this culture and its relation to American business. Hispanics, as the fastest-growing ethnic component of the American population with customs and values derived from their Latinate backgrounds, will have a substantial effect on American business as owners and managers as well as consumers. In 1980 they represented 6.4 percent of the total United States population of 227.7 million people, a 61 percent

increase from 1970. Some analysts predict that the predominantly young and highly fertile American Hispanic
population may by the year 2000 comprise 11 to 12 percent
of all United States residents. If present growth rates
continue, the Hispanic community could constitute as much
as one-seventh of the country's population within the next
quarter of a century, making it the largest of the minority
groups. Approximately two-thirds of the Spanish-speaking
population is concentrated in the "Sunbelt" states of
California, Texas, Florida, New Mexico, Arizona, and
Colorado. It is also in that area that Hispanic population
growth is the greatest. Although Texas and California
still account for 51 percent of the total Hispanic population, large numbers have settled in Arizona, where they
comprise 16 percent of the population. In that state alone
the rate of increase between 1970–1980 was 66.5 percent,
with the Hispanic population growing from 264,770 to
440,701. A large proportion of this minority group resides
in the two largest cities, Phoenix and Tucson. The
Standard Metropolitan Statistical Area (S.M.S.A.) for
Phoenix, according to the 1980 census, was 198,999 Hispanics or 13.2 percent of the population. For Tucson the
S.M.S.A. was 111,418 or 20.9 percent of the population.[3]

The growth and maturation of a Hispanic business
can clearly provide insights into the cultural aspects of
Hispanic business management. The history of Jacome's

Department Store presents, in microcosm, a reflection of a
leading Southwestern minority and its relationship to the
dominant "Anglo" majority. It serves another role as well.
To date none of the studies of department stores in the
United States have focused upon the effects of department
store development on the Western economy. Not only does
Jacome's history reflect the role of department stores in
early twentieth-century Western development, but it also
clearly illustrates problems of similar retail enterprises
throughout the United States in the latter part of the
twentieth century.[4]

Central to an understanding of Jacome's development
from 1896 to demise in 1980 is the early definition of its
internal structure and its interaction with the external
environment. It was the founder Carlos and his son Alex
who laid the foundation for Jacome's responses to the
larger economy as well as the changing local retail environment. Their decisions and their visions ultimately
determined the destiny of the enterprise which they built.

Long before their successors had to face the challenges of the twentieth-century revolution in retailing,
Carlos and Alex established the goals and basic operating
mechanisms of their business--all within the context of
later nineteenth-century cultural and technological assump-
tions. They left an indelible mark on objectives, decision

making, and company rituals. They also established lasting policies affecting such practical matters as the size of the work force, recruitment, training, wages, and benefits.

Important as they were, the internal factors do not stand alone. The external environment was a source of Jacome's threats and opportunities, its constraints and its contingencies. Conditions in the external environment not only influenced the effectiveness of the organization, its management autonomy, its problem-solving capabilities, and its organizational goals but also ultimately the survival of the organization itself.[5] External factors include technological, legal, political, economic, demographic, and cultural conditions at different time periods. They also include Jacome's task environment--those parts of the environment which were relevant or potentially relevant to goal setting or goal attainment.[6] This environment was shaped by customers, suppliers, regulatory groups, and competitors. Other external factors affecting Jacome's development were the effect of new technology upon Tucson's businesses; the role of transportation in business development; laws governing labor, taxes, zoning, and regulation of the retail industry; economic and demographic changes; and U.S. immigration policy.

Probably the most important changes in the larger environment eventually to make their marks on Tucson's retail community were the growth of shopping centers and the expansion of the various chains. Tucson's leading retailers--Levy's, Steinfeld's, Cele Peterson's, Dave Bloom and Sons, and Jacome's--used individual strategies to survive this revolution. A comparison of their strategies and an analysis of the changes this revolution brought to downtown Tucson sheds new light on the social and demographic history of a city in the thriving Sunbelt.

Of particular interest is the role culture played in the Jacome survival strategy and organizational structure. Culture is classically defined as "that complex whole which includes knowledge, belief, art, morals, law, custom, and any other capabilities and habits acquired by [human beings] as member[s] of society."[7] Culture not only creates environment but is also in constant interaction with it. Although culture thus defined provides a common framework and acts as social bond, it is a mistake to look on the Hispanic community as a homogeneous entity. As an example, the largest group within this community, Mexican-Americans, although sharing elements of a common culture and national heritage, are divided into at least four subgroups: "the Texas Mexican-American segment, the California group, the New Mexico and Colorado group, and the recently arrived Mexican group."[8] Differences among them "encompass variations in regional sub-cultures (reflecting both Mexican and Anglo components), income differences, rural and urban backgrounds, and differing

attitudes and perspectives brought by succeeding generations of immigrants." Also, because economic development
of the Southwest has varied in terms of urbanization and
industrialization, "a second generation Chicano from Texas
may still reflect a rural background whereas a California
Chicano of second generation may be an urban barrio
resident."[9]

The traditional approach taken by sociologists and
anthropologists to describe the components of Mexican-
American culture has come increasingly under attack in
recent years. Mexican-American scholars argue that "Anglo-
American social scientists have perpetuated and legitimized
simplistic stereotypes and have allowed their own cultural
biases to blind them." Although they, in turn, have determined in several instances what Mexican-American culture is
not, a model of Mexican-American culture has yet to appear.
Perhaps this is explained by the very diversity of the
group.[10]

Some agreement exists, however, on certain common
denominators such as language, and although conditioned by
a variety of factors, the critical socializing influences
of the family have endured.[11] Whether in the city for
generations or recently arrived, Tucson's Mexican-Americans
shared certain common characteristics: devotion to
Catholicism, family, and extended kinship systems; bilingualism; and a preference for distinctive foods and music.

Although the most important factor perpetuating the separate culture is family, patterns of economic, educational, language, and religion are important environmental factors as well.[12]

The part "familism" played in the development of Jacome's is of special interest. According to John Dewey, "Society exists through a process of transmission quite as much as biological life. This transmission occurs by means of communication of habits of doing, thinking, feeling from the older to the younger."[13] The patriarch of the Jacome family, Carlos, inherited many of his ideas, hopes, expectations, standards, and opinions from his ancestors in Sonora, Mexico. He in turn transmitted that cultural heritage to his sons who assumed management of the store after his death. Thus, Carlos' distinctive brand of Mexican-American culture continued to dominate not only the structural development of Jacome's but also the strategy utilized for the store's survival.

Yet it is impossible fully to understand culture as a concept whether defined as custom, tradition, norms, values, rules, or other terms without some reference to the historical formulation of cultural philosophy. Contrasting philosophical orientations of Mexican-Americans and Anglos offer some clues to the differing perspectives of the two cultures. The settlement of New England by the British almost a hundred years after Spain had settled in Mexico and South America resulted in a "splitting" of America into two major parts: Anglo-America and Hispano-America.[14] That split produced crucially different social effects. The British Reformation, the Industrial Revolution, and the developments of modern sciences which those revolutions produced spawned the Anglo-American culture. Hispano-American culture stemmed from the Hispanic Renaissance, the Catholic Reformation, and native Indian contributions.[15] Even before Anglo entry into the southwestern borderlands, these differing cultural origins provided fertile ground for Anglos to develop a negative stereotype of Mexicans. Beginning with seventeenth-century New England, they adopted the antipathy toward Catholic Spain harbored by their mother country, England. Colonists agreed with England that the Spanish government was "authoritarian, corrupt, and decadent," and that Spaniards were "bigoted, cruel, greedy, tyrannical, fanatical, treacherous, and lazy." Later this stereotype, aptly entitled the "Black Legend," combined with racism to provide Anglo-Americans with the basis for perceptions of Mexican inferiority.[16]

The influence of Catholicism basic to the philo-sophical thought of Mexico[17] is also evident in some of the cultural traits sometimes attributed to Hispanic business managers. For instance, the Church's authoritarian, hier-archical leadership style also characterizes Hispanic business management. Eschewing shared responsibility in business, Hispanic business managers prefer a highly personalized, strong leadership style and resist delegation of their authority. This authoritarian leadership style brings with it a tightly structured organizational nucleus demanding obligation to the central leader. Not unexpectedly, little time is spent on the development of successor regimes.[18]

One prominent authority concluded that "since the Latin tradition of acquiescence to a central authority is not far removed from most Hispanic experience," some Hispanics do not fight governmental interference. An acceptance of the inevitability of control of the business climate does not, however, translate into a philosophy which views the state as a benefactor. Quite the contrary: Hispanics traditionally see the state in negative terms. It exists to tax, to police one's life, to refuse requests. It is difficult for most Hispanics to visualize "el gobierno" as an agent of progress or beneficence in their lives. Their personal experience does not allow such an attitude.[19]

Hispanic business owners are particularly wary of outside control, however subtle it might be. At a fundamental level, Hispanics are inclined to believe that only by owning their businesses can they eliminate external interference. This is probably a primary reason for the preponderance of sole proprietorships in the Hispanic business community.[20]   This is probably also the reason for the tendency among Hispanic business managers to limit positions of trust to family members.   In so doing, they reduce perceived risk and increase personal control.[21]

Rather than economic return, Hispanic business owners list the driving force behind their business ventures as this desire for personal control and autonomy.[22] Another cultural trait, an active propensity to save for the future and the unexpected, has often provided the necessary capital for this "much coveted" business independence.[23]   Their attitudes regarding personal and business growth are consonant with those held by the established Anglo-dominated business community.   These include a commitment to the work ethic and a belief in the free enterprise system.[24]   Two advantages Hispanic business owners have had over their Anglo counterparts in terms of business growth internationally, however, are Spanish language competency and knowledge of Latin cultures.   These skills place the American Hispanic businessman at the forefront both in terms of communication and in knowledge of Latin American business practices.[25]

In the immediate external environment, Hispanics have "suffered discrimination in gaining access to traditional established business networks."   The formal and informal networks that are nourished in business and professional associations, social clubs, fraternal organizations, and other groups have not frequently included members of the Hispanic business community.[26] Prejudice and discrimination are deeply rooted in the ethos of American culture, and no minority group has escaped their evils. Cultural differences separating Mexican-Americans and Anglos, as well as the conditions under which Mexican-Americans became members of Tucson's society, almost guaranteed that discrimination would become part of their lives.

Carlos Jacome overcame these barriers and gained access to the inner circles of the town's business community. An understanding of the historical background of Tucson's Mexican-Americans and their Mexican origins gives a clearer picture of the obstacles he encountered while moving to the mainstream of Tucson's business life. Or as one historian so aptly put it, "Mexican history . . . is at least as essential to understanding Mexican-American history as the history of England is to understanding United States history." Indeed, because the Southwest's institutions, traditions, and beliefs have been shaped by a unique historical experience with Mexico, it is probably more essential.[27]

Carlos shared a common linkage to Mexico's past with other immigrants to Tucson whether they came from the Mexican states of Chihuahua, Sinaloa, and Jalisco or from his home state of Sonora.[28] No one is absolutely sure where this history began. It is well-known, however, that when the Spaniards arrived in 1519, Hernan Cortés found the developed Indian civilization of the Aztecs, which he conquered by 1535. The Spaniards then set about the task of Christianizing the Indians and living off the wealth of the land. During the next three centuries, multiple grievances inevitably developed in New Spain both among the subjugated Indians and the Mexican-born Spaniards. These grievances led to revolt in 1810 and to Mexico's independence in 1821. Little prepared for self-government, Mexico underwent chaotic instability which culminated in the presidency of Antonio López de Santa Anna.[29] In quick order followed Texas independence, the Mexican-American War, and the subsequent loss of territory which became the American Southwest.

Throughout the nineteenth century and part of the twentieth, disruptions in Mexico directly affected the Tucson area. Before the Treaty of Guadalupe Hidalgo, which ended the Mexican-American War, Arizona and New Mexico were part of Mexico; and the residents of Tucson were, with few exceptions, Mexican. Although only part of Arizona was gained by the Treaty, the 1854 Gadsden Purchase brought the southwestern portion, which contained Tucson, into the United States. Two years after the acquisition, the Mexican flag was replaced with the stars and stripes. Still, only a few Anglos lived in the area.[30] The Mexican population taken into the United States under these two documents "became a minority not by immigrating nor by being brought into this country as a subordinate people but by being conquered."[31]

Future events influenced migration to Tucson, including the French Intervention period in Mexico between 1861 and 1867. The war between Benito Juarez and Maximilian of Austria, the puppet of Napoleon III of France, drove many Mexican citizens across the border into Arizona. The overthrow of Porfirio Díaz in 1910 and the resulting eleven-year struggle among a number of new leaders for control of the Mexican government had a similar effect on migration.[32] Thus, Tucson's population of Mexican descent includes those whose families came to Tucson from Sonora during the French Intervention and the American Civil War and those whose parents and grandparents fled Mexico during the 1910 Revolution. It also includes a large minority whose antecedents have been in the area nearly two hundred years[33] and other more recent arrivals attracted to Tucson for various reasons, including family ties and jobs.

Yet until approximately 1880, Tucson was a place of relatively harmonious racial relations. Several of the factors cited for these friendly relations between Anglos and Mexican-Americans include threats of raids by hostile Indians, which out of necessity brought cooperation against a common and more numerous enemy of both groups--the Apache;[34] intermarriage between Anglo men and Mexican-American women, which resulted in closer interethnic relationships;[35] Mexican-American economic influence because Tucson's trade was oriented toward the neighboring state of Sonora, and the necessities of dealing with Mexican merchants and freighters enhanced the Tucson Mexican merchant's standing; Mexican-American political power, which accounted for about the only representation of the group in the Arizona legislature; and the support of Europeans in Tucson who identified with the Mexican-American community and added to that community's political strength.[36]

By 1880, Anglos controlled the city's power structure. Of the hundred-odd leading citizens who served on committees preparing for the arrival that year of the first train, only a handful had Mexican names. With the railroad came increased migration, and the new arrivals were mainly Anglos. This contributed to an increasing "Americanization" of the city. The arrival of the railroad also heavily weighted economic affairs in favor of the Anglos with their ties to large companies "back East." More significantly, the railroad brought North American women as well as men to Tucson. Interethnic marriages became rarer and cross-cultural understanding diminished.[37]

Nativism that gained support from the Panic of 1893 reinforced disintegrating relations. The nativist campaign focused on restricting immigration and "Americanizing" those immigrants already in the United States. In the Southwest, Mexicans fit the image of the undesirable immigrant. They were dark, non-European, Catholic, and had a lower living standard. This last particularly upset nativists during the depression years. They argued that because Mexicans tolerated a lower standard of living, they would take jobs away from native-born United States citizens.[38]

Ignacio Cavillo, a member of the Alianza Hispano-Americana, an organization formed to fight nativism, recalled the formation of a nativist organization in Tucson. "In those days," stated Cavillo, "the English and Spanish-speaking people had a hard time getting along. The element opposed to the Spanish-American people organized itself into the American Protective Association" (A.P.A.).[39] The most influential of the nativists' groups, the A.P.A. supported nativists' programs with political action and lobbied for legislation to restrict undesirable immigration and limit the influence of undesirable immigrants already in the United States.[40]

In fact, Carlos C. Jacome and Ignacio Cavillo were two of the founders of the Alianza Hispano-Americana in 1894. Specifically, the goals of the organization were to preserve the prestige and influence of Tucson community leaders of Mexican descent against changing circumstances.[41] Friendly relations between Mexican-Americans and others in Tucson, however, were never restored to their pre-1880 status.

In 1907 the Old Pueblo Club, which was to become the most prestigious private club for men in Tucson, was formed. No persons of Mexican descent appeared in the memberships.[42] In the same year, several prominent Anglos moved from South Main where their neighbors were Hispanics to a location to the north appropriately nicknamed "Snob Hollow."[43] Other private clubs also restricted their memberships to Anglos.[44] Restrictive covenants prohibiting Mexican settlement in Anglo residential areas characterized the documents governing some subdivisions. Later when public swimming pools were opened, Mexican-Americans were limited to swimming on Saturdays before the pool water was changed.[45]

Between 1900-1910, the Anglo population became the majority in Tucson. As more and more Anglos moved into Tucson, their economic domination increased. Although recovery from the 1893-1894 depression improved relations, the split remained. Economic downturns such as the Great Depression reemphasized this split as the scramble for jobs encouraged Anglos to resort to both informal and formal discrimination.[46]

Changes in Anglo and Mexican-American relations operated within the environmental context of a quiet but vital Tucson business life. As the farthest outpost founded by the Spanish on the Sonoran frontier, Tucson's main economic lifeline originally pointed south to Mexico City. This changed in the years following annexation by the United States. Meanwhile, although fur trappers and itinerant traders found their way to Tucson, the first American store was not opened until March 1856, when Solomon Warner engaged a pack train of fourteen mules to take 300 pounds of goods from Yuma to Tucson, where he opened a shop in the downtown area.[47]

Until the 1960s, downtown Tucson remained the focus of business and, of course, shoppers. As a result, the center of town moved very little for almost a century. In 1873, the center of town was at West Congress and Main Street. By 1954, it had moved only two blocks east from Main to Stone and one block north from Congress to Pennington.[48] Change came quickly in the 1960s, however, when the center of municipal activity moved east and north as shopping centers sprang up to service shoppers in those areas. The growth in land area contained by the city limits between 1950 and 1963 explains much of this change. In 1950, the city land area of 9.55 square miles. By 1960, it had increased to 70.96 square miles.[49]

An ethnically diverse population utilized the downtown Tucson shopping area. In 1881 the city had an estimated 10,000 people, mostly Mexican and Anglo.[50] Later, in the early 1900s, Yaqui Indians fleeing persecution in Sonora, Mexico, combined with the large Papago population to increase the number of Indians in a Tucson merchant's customer mix. Except for the Yaqui village of Pascua on East Grant Road, most of the Indians lived south of the railroad track in areas where Mexicans and a few Blacks lived.[51] Chinese, attracted to Tucson by the railroad, settled in the region between 1870 and 1900, although one large family was established in the city before the railroad arrived.[52] According to the 1870 census, nine Blacks lived in Tucson, and by 1930 there were slightly over 1,000. Their numbers grew substantially after World War II.[53]

By 1945, Anglos, Chinese, Blacks, Mexican-Americans, and Indians commingled in this downtown shopping area and patronized those retail establishments which particularly catered to their needs. Most retail stores, including specialty shops such as Dave Bloom and Sons and Cele Peterson's, made a concerted effort to employ a bilingual sales force.[54] An interesting survey of the three major department stores in 1950--Levy's, Steinfeld's, and Jacome's--revealed the following statistics on sales staffs and customer mix.[55]

SALES STAFF

	Anglo	Mexican
Jacome's	20	20
Levy's	12	4
Steinfeld's	39	7

CUSTOMERS

	Anglo	Mexican	Negro	Indian
Jacome's	38	18	7	1
Levy's	22	5	5	
Steinfeld's	35	7	1	

The growth of these department stores in the downtown Tucson business district was part of the transformation in retailing in the United States which actually dated back to the opening of the Bon Marché in Paris in 1852. Aristide Boucicaut, owner of the Bon Marché, revolutionized retailing by introducing the small mark-up in order to achieve higher sales volume and more rapid stock turnover. He also began the use of fixed and marked prices replacing individual bargaining, free entrance to the store without obligating the customer to buy (entrée libre), and the practice of allowing the customers to exchange the merchandise bought or have their money refunded. Boucicaut's success led to the broadening of operations by adding new lines. This in turn brought separate departments into the store, each corresponding to a specialty shop. The first country to follow the French example was the United States, where Steward in New York, Wanamaker in Philadelphia, and Marshall Field in Chicago popularized the department store in the 1870s.[56]

Events taking place in New England at the turn of the century augured the demise of Jacome's and other department stores locally and nationally as the twentieth century advanced. Filene's of Boston led the way with two changes foreshadowing the future development of the retail industry. First, they founded the Retail Research Association to facilitate exchange of information formerly regarded as confidential. In 1918 the Retail Research Association became the Associated Merchandising Corporation. As a result of participation in this second association, Filene's recognized the need to stabilize earnings through geographic dispersion of risk and began advocating the formation of a national retail holding company. Eventually, Filene's joined with its Associated Merchandising Corporation partners, Abraham and Strauss of Brooklyn, New York, and F. and F. Lazarus and Company of Columbus, Ohio, to form Federated Department Stores. The corporate office of this new holding company, placed in Cincinnati, Ohio, allowed each local store autonomous sales control but retained responsibility for allocating investment funds to the individual store. Thus control over expansion passed from local management to the holding company.

Another Filene activity was the development of the "Automatic Bargain Basement," in some ways the precursor of the modern discount department store. Its success in selling brand-name merchandise at discount prices encouraged other firms to adopt this revolutionary idea that would come to dominate retailing. Emerging in the 1950s, discount outlets further restructured the retailing industry by undercutting department store prices and forcing the more established retailing modes to cut costs or compete on another basis.[57]

By 1975 sales from discount department stores and a third revolutionary change in retailing, the department store chain, accounted for 89 percent of all department store sales.[58] Chains had gained momentum between 1900-1915, but their greatest expansion took place between 1940-1950. One of the factors in their continued growth and expansion was the control they held over manufacturers and vendors through their ability to purchase the largest share of an individual manufacturer's output. This was something which small retailers found impossible to do. After World War II, discount department stores, national retail holding companies, and department store chains began to supplant independent department stores. Although continuing to maintain downtown stores, these three forms of retail trade also influenced the decline of downtown shopping as they followed the population shift to the suburbs in the late 1940s.[59]

These evolutionary changes in retailing mirrored the growth of large-scale business enterprise in other sectors of the United States economy in the late nineteenth and early twentieth centuries. As in retailing, technological advances and improvements in transportation and communication made their growth possible. Geographically isolated from the center of national retailing activity, Tucson businesses enjoyed the positive benefits these changes brought. Isolation from the nation's mainstream of economic life buffered them from the negative consequences of organizational growth and consolidation until the latter part of the twentieth century. Up to that point more immediate concerns guided their day-to-day activities. In Carlos' case, growth and expansion of his retail establishment locally took precedence. His Mexican-American cultural background played an important role in that growth both in terms of the store's internal development and in its interaction with the broader Tucson environment. When he opened his store in 1896, newly married and faced with supporting a growing family, Carlos probably had only one concern as a business strategy: survival.

CHAPTER TWO

THE BEGINNINGS: "LA BONANZA, CARLOS C. JACOME, PROPRIETOR"

As soon as he became owner of "La Bonanza" in 1896, Carlos Jacome began to create the store's external and internal environments. Without abandoning his cultural origins, he established both within the store and in the outer community a strong foundation for the store's future growth. The external environment during this early period consisted primarily of downtown Tucson and included those individuals and groups important to the store's growth and survival: competitors, customers, governmental agencies, and various suppliers of capital, materials, and space.[1]

Internally, Carlos developed a rational structural environment--the formal pattern of relationships, basic operating mechanisms, stated goals, and work flow--which was complemented by the store's informal culture. Generally organizational culture is defined as that body of customary beliefs and social forms within an organization-- symbols, ideologies, language, beliefs, rituals, and myths --which are the expressive components of the organization. Pervading the organization and shaping and channeling behavior, these intangible, expressive cultural elements can either integrate with the more rational structure or rise in opposition to it. Carlos' genius in achieving the

24

former contributed not only to a sense of cohesiveness and esprit de corps among Jacome's personnel but also conveyed a congruent cultural image of the store to the broader community.[2]

Over the years, the story of Carlos' life and "La Bonanza's" early development became part of this informal culture. Taking on a myth-like quality, this story provided inspiration to store personnel while painting a vivid portrait of Jacome's beginnings for the larger community. As told and retold in newspaper articles, pamphlets, and publicity releases, it revealed in dramatic form the origin and evolution of the organization. In almost sacred terms, it depicted a man of humble origins and strong internal values whose vision and perseverance brought the store's success.[3] This approach was not unique to Jacome's. Other retailers in the downtown area pursued a similar story line when developing material for promotional purposes.

The Jacome story began in Ures, Sonora, Mexico, where Carlos was born on April 8, 1870. The family was poor, and life in Ures was difficult. Choosing to search for new opportunities elsewhere, Carlos' mother and father, Mariana and Ramon, moved their family to Magdalena, Sonora, in the early seventies. Ramon became ill there, however, and in later years Carlos recalled the frequent visits made to their ramshackle house by a man with a black satchel.[4]

After Ramon's death, Mariana gathered her children and moved to Tucson.[5]

Tucson was a growing country town when Carlos arrived. Incorporated as a village in 1871[6] and the territorial capital of Arizona, it became an incorporated city shortly after the family settled there.[7] In appearance and atmosphere, Tucson remained, however, a Sonoran town. Its principal structures were one-story, flat-roofed adobes painted in different colors. There were no paved streets, and there was little vegetation. At the heart of the town sat the imposing St. Augustine Cathedral.[8]

The principal business district of Tucson stretched from Main Street eastward to Stone Avenue. It boasted fifteen general stores, including L. Zeckendorf and Company, which occupied several buildings at the corner of Main and Congress Streets. It also had two breweries, ten saloons, two flour mills which sold grain all over Arizona, four feed and livery stables, two hotels, two jewelers, and several professional offices. Already the mixture of Hispanic and Anglo cultures was evident not only from the differing forms of dress but also from the coexistence of Spanish and English in the business district.[9]

Carlos attended school near the business district in a long, low three-room adobe building located east of St. Augustine Cathedral on Congress and Scott Streets. Opened in 1875, the Congress Street school was divided into three classes: two for primary boys and girls and one for advanced boys.   During three years of school, Carlos studied English and basic mathematics.   One of his teachers, Ingeniero Bonillas, a graduate of Massachusetts Institute of Technology, later became Ambassador to the United States from Mexico under President Carranza.   Part of the school's playground became the site of the Jacome's Department Store in 1925.[10]

    School ended for Carlos when he was nine years old. He went to work because his mother found it impossible to support the family alone.   His first job was carrying mud from the ground to the roof of a group of adobe buildings which were under construction opposite the Placita de San Agustín.   After a few days on his mud-carrying job, he caught the eye of Isadore Mayer, resident partner of L. Mayer and Company.   Mayer saw the boy struggling with his load, thought it too much for one his age, and stopped him and hired him to work for his firm.[11]

    The first retail job was as cash boy for Isadore Mayer's "California Store," a leading dry goods and cloth-ing house.[12]   This was followed by several other jobs in the retailing firms of Lonergan and Holmes and Zeckendorf's.   At Lonergan and Holmes, a popular shoe store located at Church and Congress Streets, he worked with a former schoolmate, Genero S. Manzo, later to become a trusted partner and business associate.   Spending approximately one-half of his fifteen years of employment at Zeckendorf's,[13] Carlos, like his future partner, Loreto Carrillo, and many other prominent Tucson merchants, gained much experience in retailing by working for this leading family in Western mercantile history.

The Zeckendorfs had begun their retail careers in Santa Fe, New Mexico, in 1854. Establishing connections in Tucson, they placed a permanent store there in 1869. A nephew, Albert Steinfeld, joined them in 1872 and bought the family out in 1904. As sole owner of the store, he changed the name to Steinfeld's. Although active in mining, real estate, manufacturing, banking, and hotel-keeping, Albert and later his son, Harold, made the store the center of family interests.[14] In subsequent years, Steinfeld's played an important role in the development of Jacome's Department Store.

While working for the Zeckendorfs, Carlos met Dionisia Montijo Germán, like himself born in Ures, Sonora. Part of the Jacome legend involves Dionisia's mother, Doña Trinidad Montijo Germán and the home she established in Tucson. As a rugged, self-sufficient young woman, Doña Trini, as her friends in Tucson called her, had packed her bag and taken a northbound stage from Ures to California. When she returned to Ures, richer than when she left, she bundled up her few possessions and with Dionisia moved to Tucson. In 1879, Doña Trini purchased land for a home outside the old Spanish presidio wall at 271 North Stone, across from the Tucson cemetery. Because the land was outside the wall, it was considered vulnerable to Indian attack and thus less valuable. She purchased it for a total of $400, which she paid in twenty $20 gold pieces.[15]

Carlos and Dionisia were wed in her home on May 18, 1891, and later would raise their thirteen children there.[16] All of the children grew to adulthood, an amazing record in a day of high infant mortality and in Tucson where the overall death rate for "Mexican" citizens was much higher than for those in the "American" population. For instance, the total number of deaths for "Mexicans" listed in the 1897-1898 City Directory was 98 (21.7 percent) as compared with 35 (7.7 percent) for "Americans."[17] Similarly, in 1899-1900, "Mexican" deaths totaled 166 (31.1 percent), and "American" deaths numbered 47 (8.1 percent).[18] Contributing factors to this death rate were childhood diseases such as measles, diphtheria, scarlet fever, and smallpox. Carlos, Jr., contracted diphtheria in 1893, but no other member of the family contracted it, and he recovered.[19]

After four years of marriage, Carlos and Dionisia had a family of three children, and Dionisia was pregnant again. At twenty-six, Carlos realized that as long as he worked for others, he would not command the salary needed to accommodate his responsibilities. Searching for an opportunity to become more independent, he turned to his friend, Loreto Carrillo. Loreto's father, Emilio, a pioneer Tucsonan, was a prosperous rancher east of Tucson and owned several pieces of property in Tucson. Loreto appeared financially able to undertake an independent business enterprise.[20]

Besides a growing family and increasing financial responsibilities, Carlos probably initiated business ownership for several other complex reasons all tied to his cultural background. One was the entrepreneurial spirit derived both from his immigrant experience and his Sonoran heritage. Although there are differing perspectives on immigration,[21] one view is that the act of leaving one's native country to travel to the United States requires a drive for achievement and a high tolerance for risk, traits which characterize entrepreneurs.[22] Also, several observers of Mexican culture have described Sonoran Mexicans as "different" and proud of the fact. Noted for their independence and fearless aggressiveness, Sonorans are considered more gringo-ized than other Mexicans--"mas agringado que los otros mexicanos." According to experts, Sonorans have long had a reputation as adventurers, settling in California in the late 1700s and contributing many prospectors to the California gold fields in the 1840s. Some have attributed the Sonorans' unique personality to their suffering and intermittent civil war throughout most of the nineteenth century.[23] Perhaps the policy of the Mexican government toward the region played a role as well as the enhancement of economic opportunities which the borderlands provided. The government had long sought to promote settlement in those areas bordering the United States.[24] As Frederick Jackson Turner hypothesized for the American frontier, this existence of free open territory may have been the most important factor in forming the distinctive features of Sonoran character. This is not to say that the society which developed in the borderlands was an exact replica of the American frontier. Although similarities existed between the culture of the two frontiers, the differences outweighed the similarities.[25]

Other contributing factors for Carlos' going into business may have included a drive for independence motivated by a need for security, the example set by other successful Hispanic businessmen in the Tucson area, the long-established Mexican-American community in Tucson and the solid base it offered him for going into business, and his participation in activities which gave him access to those holding positions of power and influence. A recent study of Hispanic entrepreneurs has found a high correlation between success and a desire for personal independence. In fact, this need for autonomy ranked higher as the principal factor for going into business than making

money. Often when the entrepreneur's early life was spent
in poor and difficult circumstances as in Carlos' case, the
desire for independence is coupled with "a drive to over-
come economic insecurity through personal success and an
awareness that true security could only exist" through
company ownership.[26]

Another factor, the role models of successful
Hispanic businessmen, may have contributed to Carlos'
belief in prospects of his own success. Some of those who
may have inspired him were Esteban Ochoa, Mariano
Samaniego, and Leopoldo Carrillo. All three were
freighters. Ochoa also owned a stage line and several
retail stores for which he secured additional business
through government contracts to carry the mail and supply
the military. Leopoldo Carrillo was well known in the area
for Carrillo's Gardens, a place where townspeople could
find recreation outside the saloons. He was regarded as a
man who seldom let a "dollar slip through his fingers."[27]
That these men had prospered in Tucson gave evidence of the
support offered by the solidly established Mexican community. Because of the community, as well, positions of
influence were available to persons of Hispanic background.
Probably Carlos' election to one of these positions, a
director on the board of the Tucson Building and Loan
Association early in 1895, was a deciding reason for opening a business. As a director he had access to needed

expertise in business transactions and the contacts and knowledge to borrow money, perhaps even the $300 which he and Loreto each invested to open the store.[28]

On March 18, 1896, just nine days after the birth of his fourth child, Carlos joined Loreto in opening "La Bonanza." When the store opened, Tucson's population was 8,000 and included fifteen lawyers, four physicians, three dentists, and three photographers. The town already had several dry goods stores, including Zeckendorf's, W. F. Kitt, Meyer's Bee Hive, W. E. Felix, and Gandolfo and Sanguinetti.[29] Yet, except for Zeckendorf's, which later became Steinfeld's, Jacome's was the only dry goods store of that era to survive. The partners picked March as the most auspicious month for opening because of the potential attraction of customers. Zeckendorf's, for example, "catered to the spring buying for the mines and ranches, holding elaborate public affairs each March to attract crowds--and customers."[30] Born with the opening of "La Bonanza" was a competitive-cooperative relationship between these two Tucson retail enterprises which lasted throughout much of the twentieth century.

The new partners had picked a good time to start "La Bonanza." Tucson was coming out of a long business recession in 1896[31] and moving into a period of time when independent retailers in the city and elsewhere would enjoy their greatest development. It was a time when the profits of that era of prosperity could be channeled back into the business without the central government or state or city treasuries claiming a large proportional tribute.[32]

Enhancing Carlos' and Loreto's expectations of success were changes which had taken place in Tucson since the arrival of the railroad in 1880. Its coming had increased the town's growth and development east and west, which broke the old north-south pattern, while migration of Anglos multiplied the number of available customers. Although the growing Americanization of the city had also changed building styles, with inflammable lumber replacing the fire-resistant adobe as a building material, the partners could depend on protection from a fire department created in 1883.[33] Other technological changes enhancing business growth included introduction of a telephone exchange in 1881, gaslights in 1882,[34] a municipal water system in the same year,[35] and an electric company in 1895.[36] The store's out-of-town shoppers could stay at the newly remodeled Cosmopolitan Hotel at Pennington and Main Streets which reopened in December of 1896 with "hot and cold bathrooms on every floor."[37]

Until the arrival of the railroad, there was no need for vehicular transportation within the town. With the developed area measuring about a mile at its broadest points north and south, most residences were within two or three blocks of the heart of the business district. With the railroad about three-quarters of a mile uphill from the main business district, there was suddenly a need to connect the two with public transportation.[38]   For those customers or suppliers needing such transportation to "La Bonanza," small owner-operated enterprises filled this void the first year of the store's operation.   In 1897, a permanent transit system in the form of the Tucson Street Railway replaced this small owner system, and by 1898 mule-drawn streetcars connected the downtown area with the University of Arizona.[39]

Still, to those less optimistic than the two partners, Tucson was a provincial and backward place with little apparent potential for long-term business development.   The streets were unpaved, many of the adobe houses uninhabitable, and the moral atmosphere "far from bracing."[40]   Gambling was a major occupation, open prostitution flourished, and the all-night saloon was legal until 1908.[41]

Carlos became a member of one group pushing for Tucson's development, the Tucson Chamber of Commerce, organized in 1896. Publishing the first promotional literature describing the city's assets, it also established the Sunshine Climate Club in 1922 with Carlos as one of the founders.   This club had the sole purpose of attracting tourists to Tucson.[42]

Throughout these changes in early twentieth-century Tucson, "La Bonanza" and later Jacome's structural development bore the imprint of Carlos' Hispanic background and culture. The organizational structures, processes, and norms Carlos "imprinted" during the store's creation tended to persist even though conditions in the external environment changed dramatically.[43] Internally, for example, the simple organizational structure of the store was characterized by a centralized locus of decision-making authority which, according to a recent authority on Hispanic business management, corresponds to Hispanic leadership style.[44] From the beginning, Carlos, described by his son, Augustine, as the "dean" of the business, participated in every aspect of the store's operation. This ranged from dealing with Indian customers to serving as the store's only buyer. According to Augustine, even the Papago Indians considered him a chief, coming to him with their problems and often leaving a wagon load of mesquite wood in payment.[45] This firm view of the executive leadership role persisted with Carlos' son and successor, Alex, Sr., whose favorite phrase was "only one captain."[46]

Like the Southern country store owner and some of the Jewish retailers found in the downtown business district,[47] Carlos maintained a personalized approach to customer relations as well. He never allowed himself to have an office, for he believed it was his job to be on the floor at all times, greeting customers, attending to their needs, and making sure they were given the best possible service.[48] In a similar vein, the *Arizona Daily Star* noted at the time of his death, "It was a common sight in his busy store to see him stop in his work and talk and listen with some grey-haired Mexican woman or man and then without the knowledge of anyone contribute his help and advice."[49]

Carlos did have two partners in the early years of the business, Loreto Carrillo, from 1896-1903, and Genero S. Manzo, from 1902-1913. What emerges from a study of the business during this period, however, is the portrait of Carlos as leader with Loreto and later Genero giving support to his decisions. At no time, either through interviews with employees and customers or in reviewing the store's documents and newspaper clippings, did a "shared leadership" role emerge. In fact, the evidence shows that Carrillo was a cattleman with little interest in retail business.[50] Carlos as decision maker fits with his Mexican-American background because "shared responsibility is simply not a traditional part of the Hispanic manner of doing business."[51]

Carlos developed store policies which were as important in attracting customers as they were in motivating and inspiring employees. The most important of these policies were friendliness, customer satisfaction, and honesty.[52] The policy of strict truthfulness was particularly important in an era characterized by the popular warning of the age, "Let the buyer beware." While Loreto was still his partner, he set a policy of accepting returned merchandise when it was faulty. This bothered veteran horse trader Carrillo who told Carlos, "You're going to go broke doing that."[53]   Carlos also refused to carry "seconds" or inferior merchandise. This commitment was even printed on the order blanks for salesmen. It stated that "any seconds or defective goods will be returned at your expense." Integrity governed Carlos' relationship with the "drummers" as well. Overdue bills he explained with a partial payment and a note such as "I am going to be a little late with the full amount due because of a new baby in the family."[54]

In the beginning, Carlos sold nothing but staples. Because many customers shopped once a year to stock up on clothing, that stock remained about the same from year to year. Staples consisted of nothing but the essentials: quantities of calico, wool dress goods, shirts, pants, hats, overalls, socks, dresses, corsets, underwear, shoes, sheets, blankets, and towels. Customers had a choice of two or three styles at most.[55]

In a time when advertising was not common beyond the Wards and Sears catalogues reaching Tucson's homes and a few patent medicine ads in the local newspapers, Carlos developed a unique way of promoting his wares. He placed them on the plank sidewalk outside the store except when it rained and protected them from the sun by canvas. Stressing that merchandise well presented was half sold, he displayed trousers on a rack and strung men's shirts of various hues across the store's front. Other articles such as traveling bags, men's clothing samples, and women's ready-to-wear he placed on either side of the doorway.[56]

"La Bonanza's" interior, like country stores found in the southern part of the United States during the same period,[57] reflected an indifference to orderly stock keeping. Highly specialized departments were unknown at the time, and Carlos made no attempt to segregate the different classes of merchandise. The walls were lined with shelves. Everything inside the store was placed on these shelves with the leftover space filled with empty boxes to make the stock look more complete.[58] Yard goods were a major sales item for "La Bonanza," and checks, calicos, plaids, and muslins were stacked from the ceiling to the tops of the shelves. All along the back wall, goods were hung for better visibility.[59] Women loved this feature of the store, and from the beginning shopped there because it offered the best selection of yardage in town.[60] For example, a 1924 sales ticket for one of its first and best customers, Ramona Figueroa, lists primarily cotton flannel and various ribbon and lace trimmings for a total bill of $13.96.[61] Carlos spoke Papago, an added enticement for

Indian women to come to the store to buy cloth to make
their long skirts.[62]

By 1900, the interior of the store was changing,
and a more orderly appearance was taking form. The shirts
strung across the front of the store as well as other goods
originally displayed outside had been transferred to the
interior. Now, mantillas, ladies' gaily striped stockings,
lace curtains, aprons, and other bits of wearing apparel
were all hung high above the customer's heads on lines
stretched from one wall to the other. Smaller items of
merchandise such as socks, gloves, and handkerchiefs were
now hung in large bunches, and a customer could select his
or her size and color and just pull it loose from the
hanging display. Young Alex Jacome used number fifty
thread to sew the articles onto the hanging display.
Overall, even though the floor space was enlarged, the
store had a more crowded appearance due to the fact that
many articles had been added to the stock.[63]

The first change of location came in 1902 when the
store had grown sufficiently to warrant a larger space.
The business district at that time centered around Meyer
and Main Streets, but Carlos sensed Tucson's growth in
another direction, so he chose his new location at 90 West
Congress Street. At about the same time as the move,
Loreto, in ill health, sold his partnership interest to

Genaro S. Manzo. The store was renamed Jacome and Manzo. Loreto died shortly thereafter.[64]

Like Carlos, Genaro was born in Ures, Sonora, Mexico. A partner with Estevan Ochoa in a grocery store, bar, and contracting business for a number of years, Genaro joined Carlos soon after Ochoa's death. Noted in later years for his dislike of adding machines, Manzo added figures with one sweep of his pencil, a special skill he brought to his chief job as bookkeeper. He also waited on customers and did other odd jobs as the need arose.

Manzo found the store's credit procedures very haphazard. When credit was extended to Mexican and Indian customers, for example, payment in many instances was based on barter in corn, wood, watermelons, or frijoles. There was no merchant credit association and no way of checking on a person asking for credit except through another merchant on a personal basis. This was one of the reasons for high credit losses during this early period, with external causes which as crop failure or lack of rain also partly to blame.[65]

Jacome and Manzo remained partners in business until 1913, at which time Manzo sold his interest in the store to Carlos. He left Tucson for five years of ranch life, but when the 1918 drought all but wiped out his holdings, he was compelled to return to Tucson. He then became credit manager and auditor for the store and remained a trusted employee until his death in 1954.[66]

The partners found in 1907 that the nationwide depression after a decade of prosperity made "La Bonanza" to quote Alex, Sr., "anything but."[67] Yet, the firm expanded before recovery occurred into adjoining quarters at 86 West Congress with a lease of $125 per month. As Carlos' son, Alex, recalled in 1957, "In the sixty-one years Jacome's has been in business there have been three depressions that paralyzed commerce in this country--shocks that came in 1907, 1921, and of course 1929. For some reason which I can't explain Jacome's has taken each of these occasions to expand."[68] Perhaps cultural conditioning played a role wherein the Jacomes set aside a certain amount of their profits for the future and the unexpected. As a result, the business could grow during times of national economic downturns with fewer distractions from reduced competition.[69]

With the expansion in 1907, the stock could be arranged with more order and displayed more advantageously. Gas light fixtures added a modern touch, and a long ladder which ran around the room on a guide provided easier access to the stock, which was stacked to the top of the very high ceiling. A sample of everything in the store was crowded into the four windows of the store in a rather hit-or-miss fashion. By 1910, the interior took on still more order as

show cases were added.[70] Women were now part of the sales
force. One of the first saleswomen, Elina Sayre, recalled
her boss, Carlos, with deep affection as a "father figure
who taught her how to work."[71]

The Tucson central business district was expanding
and changing right along with "La Bonanza." Out-of-town
customers could now stay at the two-hundred-room Santa Rita
Hotel which opened at Broadway and Scott in 1904.[72] Paved
streets appeared in 1911 when Stone Avenue was macadamized,
and asphalt paving was begun in 1913, although for many
years the business district was the only paved area in
Tucson.[73] As early as 1903, those driving the new mode of
transportation, the automobile, encountered a speed limit
of seven miles per hour,[74] and two years later they had to
have a driver's license.[75]

New businesses were also appearing. In 1906, Dave
Bloom, Sr. and Cress Myers founded the Savings Bank Store
at 17 North Stone Avenue. Like Carlos, Bloom had worked
for the firm founded by the Zeckendorf brothers. One of
his favorite stories was about a two-week trial stint with
Albert Steinfeld. He volunteered his services for nothing,
"updated" the men's inventory so that only he knew where
everything was located, and through these efforts, at the
end of the two-week period was the best men's-wear salesman
Steinfeld's had. Known in the mercantile language of the
day as "a racket store," which meant it carried small

inexpensive items similar to a five-and-dime, over five years Bloom and Myers gradually changed to men's wear. In 1911 they moved the store, renamed Myers and Bloom, to Congress Street when a banker offered them a loan of $45,000 to buy out a local firm on the edge of bankruptcy.[76]

Like the Jacome's the Bloom family, as part of the first generation of Tucson merchandising families, was central to downtown business growth for much of the twentieth century. Although the Bloom enterprise remained a specialty shop while the Jacome business evolved into a department store, the Blooms were pleased to have the Jacome store in their vicinity as a "complementary" competitor attracting potential customers to their store. Each business stressed personalized attention to customers, but Mexican customers found the Jacome's proficiency in Spanish an added enticement. Each store was family-owned and family-operated. As leadership of each store changed hands, however, it was apparent that decision making at the Bloom store was shared with compromise characterizing the final outcome, whereas a hierarchical decision-making process prevailed at the Jacome enterprise. Too, with the passing years, Jacome personnel contained many more family members than did Bloom's and other family-owned enterprises in downtown Tucson, including Steinfeld's and Levy's.[77]

By the second decade of "La Bonanza's" existence, largely through Carlos' efforts, it was gaining status in the community not only through innovative advertising techniques but most importantly through Carlos' many activities which brought him in contact with people important to the store's development. New advertising approaches included colorful and crowded display windows, newspaper ads, and special promotional gimmicks. One of the special events he staged was the visit of a well-known comic strip character, Buster Brown, and his dog, Tige, for Tucson youngsters in 1910.[78] Special dishes and coin purses advertising the store were also given to the customers. Plain white with a rim of color, the dishes had embellished upon them, "La Bonanza, Carlos C. Jacome, Proprietor." Below this caption and in Spanish, a description extolled the store's merchandise. Provided by Walkover Shoes, the coin purses bore a similar inscription on the inside flap as well as a general description of the store's wares.[79]

It was Carlos' musical talents which first attracted public notice. If "music is a true expression of Mexico,"[80] Carlos more than expressed the ideal. Often, Elina Sayre remembered his deep baritone voice saying, "Come, Elina, let us go to Mass and sing."[81] His vocal talent gained him local press coverage in 1893 when the *Arizona Daily Star* noted that "Charles Jacome would sing

'Il Trovatore' at a vocal and instrumental concert to be held the following Saturday at the Opera House."[82] He also mastered the baritone horn and played in the Tucson Philharmonic Band.

Carlos also found time to participate in the Pioneer Historical Society, the Tucson Chamber of Commerce, the Sunshine Climate Club, the Sociedad Alianza Hispano-Americana, and the Arizona Constitutional Convention. Through these community activities, he accomplished an important task in terms of the store's development and survival. By gaining full participation in majority activities, he had free access to positions of power and influence without losing the unique social and cultural characteristics so important for customer attraction and retention.

Innately, he appeared to know that political participation would not only give him social legitimacy and power within the community but would also provide him a means to change conditions to his advantage.[83] True, he declined to run as the Republican nominee for City Council in 1905, but realism probably played a role in that decision because Hispanics rarely won election to the Council. The Tucson City Directory shows that few Hispanics held any public office in the state, city, or county between 1881-1950, when the listing of government officials ended. A 1961 study found that this trend had continued,

with persons of Mexican descent not proportionately represented in the influential cadre of the community.[84]

Yet, Carlos set a pattern of political involvement
which was later emulated by his son and successor, Alex.
First came his association with the Sociedad Alianza
Hispano-Americana. Mexican-Americans had been finding an
increasingly hostile climate in Tucson, precipitated
initially by the economic depression following the Panic of
1893 and afterward fed by growing nativism all across the
United States. The Alianza had been organized as a response to this changing social environment. The idea for
the Alianza had sprung from the political club called "La
Union," formed in 1893 in response to Mexican-American
unemployment and increased Anglo discrimination. At the
January 14, 1894, meeting, the name was changed to Sociedad
Alianza Hispano-Americana. When the lodge incorporated
under the laws of the territory as a fraternal benefit
society in December of 1902, Carlos was one of the seven
incorporators.[85] The Alianza made plans to build its
headquarters building in Tucson for all the lodges, and in
July, 1907, Carlos displayed the plans and model of the
front of the Alianza Hall in one of his show windows. When
the cornerstone was finally laid for the Hall on March 19,
1916, Carlos was designated by the Supreme President, who
resided in Los Angeles, as his personal representative.[86]

Republican Party concern over disfranchisement of non-English-speaking voters of Mexican descent also led to Carlos' candidacy as a delegate to the Arizona Constitutional Convention which preceded Arizona's change from territorial status to the forty-eighth state. According to *The Tucson Citizen*, July 5, 1910, "the Democrat leaders in both houses of Congress worked early and late . . . to disfranchize (sic) the Mexican voters of the territory who cannot speak English to the satisfaction of election boards."[87] Expecting Democratic politicians in the territory to carry on the fight, the *Citizen* urged the local Republicans to address the issue. At the primaries held on August 8, Carlos was one of five Republicans selected.[88]

Just two days later on August 10, the *Citizen* stated "Carlos C. Jacome is one of Pima County's leading Spanish American citizens. He is intelligent and alert, a successful businessman and a good citizen. He will be . . . a strong factor in the constitutional convention." When the general election was held on September 12, the election was overwhelmingly Republican.[89]

It was also in 1910 that the troubles in Mexico which preceded World War I drew Carlos into another color-ful event of Tucson's history, a precursor of the family's hemispheric business relations. Porfirio Diaz was deposed and many of his supporters fleeing Mexico came to Tucson.

Succeeding revolutions produced more exiles, and "La Bonanza" became a congregating place for many of these. One was General Julian Medina, who served under Pancho Villa in the State of Jalisco. Others included General Juan Cabral and Gabriel Corella, an industrialist whose son, Gabriel, Jr., worked at "La Bonanza."[90] Due to the small numbers settling permanently in Tucson, these revolutionary exiles as well as others immigrating from Mexico during this period probably had little effect upon the political orientations of Tucson's Mexican elite.[91]

Throughout the First World War, Carlos continued to expand, laying a strong foundation based on his cultural origins and business acumen for the store's future. Boom prices following the war, with gasoline selling for 36 cents a gallon[92] and food costs soaring out of sight in Tucson,[93] only spurred the store's growth. During the post-war boom period, 1919-1920, "La Bonanza" sold overalls at $4.00 a pair and shirts at $15.00.[94] Lying beneath the surface, however, were economic and social conditions which portended a changing "La Bonanza" in the coming decade.

CHAPTER THREE

THE GROWTH: JACOME'S DEPARTMENT STORE

"La Bonanza's" growth between 1896-1920 was a credit to Carlos Jacome's management style. This growth was enhanced by the absence of governmental interference either in the form of price controls or taxation. The rising purchasing power of the store's customers also helped capital accumulation. Families during this era had more available money than in later decades because they had at their disposal the accumulated savings of former generations and also habitually lived within their incomes. Traditional values continued to influence their buying habits. These included "a Puritan tradition of abstinence which made . . . free spending a sin . . . and the rigorous saving and paying of cash for everyday needs."[1] Yet, the shift from production to consumption which began after Reconstruction was accelerating as American inventiveness combined with technology, mass production, and mass marketing to produce and make available more and more goods.

What became apparent to Carlos and other merchants in downtown Tucson as well as nationwide as the 1920s advanced was the effect this abundance of material goods had upon customer attitudes and values. As described by Herbert Hoover's Research Committee on Social Trends in

1933, replacing the traditional attitudes and values of an earlier era was "increased secularization of spending . . . a new attitude which encouraged liberal spending to make the wheels of industry turn . . . a new attitude toward hardship as a thing to be avoided by living in the here and now . . . the utilizing [of] installment credit and other devices to telescope the future into the present."[2] Advertising and new forms of credit encouraged customers to buy their wants as well as their needs, and they increasingly took on financial responsibilities which in the past had been relegated to big ticket items such as furniture and pianos. One student of credit expansion during this period estimated "that the proportion of total retail sales made on credit increased from 10% in 1910 to 50% in 1929 with the volume of outstanding family credit in 1929 placed at more than 11 billion dollars."[3] Interestingly, Carlos himself continued to adhere to the old values, never borrowing against family resources for business expenses, a practice later emulated by his son, Alex.[4]

Increasingly during the 1920s Carlos worked to attract customer attention through sales promotions and attractive window and interior displays. No longer did he stock merchandise just to meet demand. As shopping and consuming became an American pastime, he began to display in large quantities to entice shoppers who had no need or intention of buying. With Arizona enjoying a particularly rapid increase in banking credit,[5] he was careful to implement credit policies which protected the store. Criteria for credit included ability to pay, standing in the community, and moral character. Apparently the reputation of an individual applying for credit was very important, and both Carlos and Alex turned down applicants who had "tainted money."[6]

Between 1920-1930, the Jacome business expanded and prospered. This despite the fact that the 1920-1921 recession, labor union problems, increased competition, and the 1929 stock market crash caused deep ripples in the heretofore placid environment of commercial Tucson. The store survived the 1920-1921 economic downturn, but many others did not. What apparently made the difference was the reserve capital Carlos had built up in the boom years following World War I.

When deflation hit Tucson in 1921, the older Jacome children were out of school and working regularly for the store. "La Bonanza" was caught with high-priced merchandise which Carlos was unwilling to sell for less. In addition, chain stores were underselling the local merchants. Penney's, for example, was selling overalls at $1.49 because the wholesale price had dropped to $1.12 a pair and the chain store could take advantage of it. Literally caught with his trousers up, Carlos found the situation especially difficult because hundreds of his customers were Southern Pacific employees who bought a lot of overalls. He finally gave in and dropped "La Bonanza's" price to $2.59 a pair, but the competition continued to attract their Southern Pacific trade.[7]

Problems "La Bonanza" encountered during this recession, however, were minimal when compared with other pioneer businesses. W. F. Kitt and Son, Ryland and Zipf, Drachman's Shoe Store, the Yellow Front, the Blue Front, Juan Grijalva's, and others were forced to close.[8] When the Kitt firm failed, Fred J. Steward of the Southern Arizona Bank and Trust Company called Carlos and suggested he take over the store located at the northeast corner of Congress and Scott, where the Congress Street school had stood. Carlos' business was $40,000 in debt at the time, but Steward offered to lend him $20,000 more. Hesitant to assume an additional debt, Carlos turned for advice to his son, Alex, a student majoring in business at The University of Arizona. According to Alex, his reply was an unqualified yes. He added, "If we go broke we may as well do so in style."[9]

When Carlos assumed control of W. F. Kitt and Sons, he moved to the other side of Stone Avenue--from 86-90 West Congress to 87-93 East Congress. It was a major change for the store because it meant a possible loss of old customers. As a precaution, he kept "La Bonanza" open as a branch store with its own manager and one assistant. He also kept several of the W. F. Kitt employees to work in the new store. One of these, Enriqueta Martinez DeMeester, clearly remembered the day Carlos took over the store. Dressed in a black suit which emphasized his strong features, blue eyes, and the redness of his complexion, he explained the transition to the Kitt employees. Enriqueta recalled thinking on that occasion about his reputation for honesty. Apparently her grandfather, Jesus Maria Martinez, who owned a ranch where the Hughes Aircraft plant was later built, had used Carlos as a bank. Everyone in those days either had a "trusted friend" in town or else they had to bury their money. So when her grandfather came to town, he left his funds with Carlos and then drew on them.[10]

The day Carlos took over, the Kitts removed the account books for the store. Shortly afterwards Enriqueta found she had the short-term responsibility of setting up the accounts. Purchasing some notebooks at Kress' dime store, she began putting in a new accounting system. A few weeks later when Jacome and his bookkeeper, Manzo, came to ask her questions about the accounts, they found she had identified each person having credit with the store with a drawing detailing his occupation. For instance, a boot and a leg stood for bootlegger. Manzo transferred these drawings to a larger ledger.[11]

Jacome's Department Store was now the name of the business located at 87-93 East Congress. Whereas "La

Bonanza" continued to have few departments, Carlos began to build on the departmentalization which W. F. Kitt had begun. The new department heads, enthusiastic about their assignments, sought to make improvements. Yet, improvement also meant change because Jacome's was catering to a new group of customers. Whereas "La Bonanza" had attracted primarily Mexican-American customers, W. F. Kitt and Sons had catered largely to Anglos. Now as the two groups converged on the store, Carlos found he was buying two types of stock to suit the demands of each group. He was also keeping a much closer watch on the inventory and integrating catalogue buying and telephone sales into the store's practices.[12]

The move across Stone Avenue meant the loss of some Papago Indian customers.[13] As a result, Mr. Wilson, the department head of dry goods, stopped buying the cloth Papago women used to make their long skirts. Yet, a few Indian customers continued venturing to the new address. One Sunday in 1925, Augustine Jacome was working on the balcony which overlooked the first floor of the store. He noticed two Indian women looking in the front door. Curiosity finally brought him to the door to find out what they wanted. Presenting him with an old Stetson hat which had belonged to their father, they requested a duplicate new one to place on their father's head before he was buried. Years later, Alex, Sr., recalled his father holding up a piece of merchandise that had remained on the shelf for months or even years and saying, "Boys, there is always a customer for every item. We've just got to find that customer."[14] Carlos' training in this case paid off because Augustine went to the stockroom and found exactly the same hat, several years old by then. The women came back again and again to thank him.[15]

On the first day, the total sales in the new store amounted to $60. On the second day the total was $98. The third day, a Saturday, it was $129. On Sunday, Carlos announced a giant sale in the newspapers, and on Monday alone he grossed $18,000.[16] People jammed into the store to buy out the old Kitt stock and look over the new Jacome surroundings. One employee, working as cashier, remembers the wire baskets, which had replaced the cash boy, moving back and forth on a network of cables between her office on the balcony and the different departments on the first floor. The only interruption in this constant movement was when something was wrong with the account. Then the cashier held the basket as a signal to the clerk below that the customer was a bad credit risk.[17]

It became more obvious after the move to Scott and Congress that customer demands were changing. With the growth of national advertising and distribution, the value of a brand name mounted steadily, with the customer shifting at an accelerated pace from one brand to another.

There was also increased interest in styles and colors, which in turn speeded up obsolescence. Although small cities in the West like Tucson lagged somewhat behind, chain stores were finding increasing success in rapidly disseminating new fashion merchandise across the country and into those out-of-the-way areas.[18]

In the words of Alex Jacome, Sr., "As the years went by merchandising . . . changed. Manufacturers started to advertise and the public became aware of brand names. More and more items appeared on the market. Tucson's housewives became style-conscious, and they began showing as much knowledge of fabrics and thread count as some of our best sales people." All of this put a new risk into doing business--the risk of ordering too much of the wrong style and seeing the merchandise left unsold on the shelves.[19] Shortly after the new store opened, Carlos was faced with just such a problem. A department manager made a mistake in the number of comforters he ordered. He had intended to order one dozen; instead Jacome's received one gross. At $35 apiece it took some time to sell 144 down comforters in the desert town of Tucson.[20]

Now Jacome's management began to meet with buyers weekly to discuss problems, sudden style changes, and the quickly changing customer demands. Consumer requests for new products was also changing Carlos' marketing practices. He disposed of slow-moving merchandise quickly and ordered fresh stocks to increase sales and profits. Buyers explained the advantages and disadvantages of new items to the sales people. Service became more important, not only as part of sales but through such additions as credit (usually short-term--thirty days), delivery service, and the handling of nationally advertised brands. By 1929, such universally well-known names carried by Jacome's besides the old standby, Stetson hats, included Butterfield patterns, Adler Collegian clothes, Walk-Over shoes, B.V.D. underwear, Headlight Overalls (union made), Indestructo trunks, and Rodeo brand riding breeches, overalls, and shirts.[21] Customer credit imposed new work schedules for some employees. Gilbert Martinez, who had begun to work in the credit office with his sister Enriqueta in 1928, remembered preparation of the bills starting on the twenty-fifth day of each month. Sometimes under the direction of Manzo, they worked until eleven or twelve o'clock at night to get the bills out by the end of the month.[22]

New promotional devices accompanied this desire to meet shifting consumer needs. Emulating its European counterparts, Jacome's advertised semi-annual sales in January and June. The store also inaugurated a spring fashion show featuring local models in 1928 to promote Butterfield patterns. By 1929, it had switched to professional models from Los Angeles. Among them was dark-haired beauty, Miss Ruth Hurscler, "awarded the prize for having the most perfect back at the 1928 national Chiropractors convention in San Francisco," and "true blonds of the most perfect type, Miss Edward and Miss Lorraine." An additional attraction was a six-year-old local pupil of the Cumberpatch Ballet School, Merilyn McCurdy. Billed as "Baby Ruth Sunshine," Merilyn "completely won those who saw her with her charming little manner and her brunette beauty."[23]

Always conscious of the store's exterior image, Carlos took pains to have attractive display windows at the new location. One Sunday, on his way to church, he noticed a large crowd gathered around one of the windows. At first he thought it was a fire, but as he drew closer he heard large peals of laughter. Looking inside, he saw the manager of men's wear, Charlie Urquides, changing the display. Because of the hot Tucson weather, hairy-chested Charlie had taken off his shirt and tie and "looked like an orangutan."[24] Afterwards, a new store policy dictated covered windows when changes took place.

This growing promotional sophistication represented a more advanced stage in Jacome's overall development. Incorporation also reflected this trend. In 1923, Carlos had incorporated with assets of $500,000. In 1928, he reincorporated and made each of the thirteen children owners of the business. Carlos continued as president and general manager with S. S. Manzo as secretary and Alexander

Jacome as treasurer.[25]   Incorporation diverged from the
typical legal structure characterizing Hispanic businesses
in the United States.   As late as 1977, the United States
Bureau of the Census survey of minority-owned business
enterprises revealed that corporations accounted for only 2
percent of the total number of Hispanic firms in the country.   Most of those firms owned by Hispanics were characterized as sole proprietorships.   The explanation lies in
the "strong drive within the culture to control one's
business endeavors."[26]

Another aspect of this incorporation process,
inclusion of family members, more closely reflected traditional Hispanic values.   There is a tendency within the
culture to limit positions of trust to family members to
reduce perceived risk and increase personal control, and if
a business does incorporate, it is usually a closely held,
family-owned entity.[27]   Yet, the characteristic of a family-owned and controlled business is not uniquely Hispanic,
having prevailed in America until the 1890s[28] and still
characterizing many businesses across the United States
today.   Family-owned firms are still prevalent in European
countries where "family roots are deeper and family traditions stronger."[29]   On the American scene a prime example
is the DuPont Company, founded in the 1800s by a prominent
French immigrant.   During its first one-hundred years
(1802-1902), that firm "might well be considered a model or

an almost ideal type of a family firm." During that time period, the needs and values of the DuPont family took precedence over the larger and impersonal demands of the enterprise. When possible, "sons or sons-in-law were recruited to head the firm with managerial selection based as much on family relationship as on ability, intelligence or business performance."[30] Only when the technological, administrative, and financial requirements of the growing business eroded family control did separation of family from business occur.[31] Within a short time of its incorporation in 1899,[32] DuPont began the metamorphosis from family firm to the modern corporation with its impersonalized approach to decision making, goal setting, and managerial selection. Distribution of stock to persons outside the family began in 1904 when important employees were allowed to purchase stock in the company.[33] In contrast to DuPont, Jacome's continued a personalized approach to corporate control from 1928 until it closed in 1980.[34] Of course, when compared with DuPont, Jacome's represented business corporate growth on a small scale, but in terms of strategic planning it faced many problems similar to those encountered by DuPont as the twentieth century advanced, especially when dealing with growth and expansion.

At an early age all nine Jacome boys--Carlos, Jr., Henry, Ramon, Juan, Frank, Alex, Arthur, Richard, and Augustine--began assuming responsibilities at the store.

As Alex, Sr., recalled in 1965, "As soon as we were old
enough to ride a bicycle, we were old enough to sweep the
floor, deliver packages and messages, mark and arrange
merchandise, and 'sell socks.'"[35] After the boys started
school, they spent their spare time and vacations in the
store. Often they spent Sundays after church getting ready
for Monday. The youngest of the thirteen children,
Augustine, remembers helping in the summers when he was not
going to school, delivering packages on his bicycle and
working in the stock room. He loved to work in the basement of "La Bonanza" despite the fact that rats had taken
up residence there. Carlos took care of the rodent problem
by making a lasso of heavy wrapping string, tying it to a
rat caught alive in a trap, and banging its head against a
telephone pole.[36]

In 1914, Carlos' sixth child, Henry, was the first
to work full-time at the store. At one point, he assumed
managerial duties on an emergency basis. Pope Pius X had
died while Carlos was in the East on a buying trip. Carlos
had left an employee, Jesus Maria Reyes, in charge of the
store. Learning of the Pope's demise, Jesus and another
employee, Benedicto Araiza, a veteran of the Mexican revolutions, locked the store's doors and took off in mourning
to drown their sorrows in one bar after another. Two days

later the store was still closed, and fifteen-year-old Henry had to reopen it.[37]

Rather than participating in the store's operation, Dionisia followed the cultural pattern of becoming the center of the home. She, together with the four Jacome girls, Anita, Sarah, Josephine, and Rose, cleaned the house and cooked for the large family. In these roles, they played a pivotal role in the store's development since both mother and daughters performed work which helped to raise the family's status. Not only did their homemaking skills significantly reduce family demands for capital which was then channeled back into the store's development, but they also maintained the family and its surroundings in a fashion highly valued by others holding power and status in the community.[38] Further, when the time came to "tighten belts at home" due to economic hard times, their skills alleviated this process.

Carlos encouraged the expanding sales force also to consider themselves as part of a family. He provided many hours outside the store for employees to get together. There were store picnics at Sabino and Bear Canyons, where Carlos would lead the group in singing such songs as "Cielito Lindo" and "Adelita." After closing on Saturday nights, he treated the men employees to menudo, enchiladas, and tamales. On Sundays, he would take a carload to Nogales, Sonora, to watch a bullfight.[39] Furthermore, he made his employees feel comfortable about coming to him for help when they encountered problems in their personal lives.[40]

By 1929, the personnel of the store had grown to thirty-five. Four Jacome boys--Alex, Henry, Ramon, and Richard--worked for the store full-time. The store had ten departments which included dry goods, hosiery, art and lingerie, ribbons/lace/notions, ladies' ready-to-wear, men's furnishings and luggage, men's hats, shoes, office, and advertising. Each department had a manager and most had an assistant. The demand for ready-to-wear was increasing each year, and various department heads like Elina Sayre of ladies' ready-to-wear made a yearly trip to the West Coast for new merchandise. Carlos and Alex visited the eastern markets twice a year to purchase the latest styles for Tucson customers.[41]

Also in 1929, Carlos sold the "La Bonanza" property at 86 West Congress and permanently closed the store. He also sold the property where the store had earlier expanded and which now housed Díaz Pelido Brothers, Jewelers.[42] Carlos' property had greatly increased in value due to the development of two new "skyscrapers" in the vicinity, the Consolidated National Bank and the Pioneer Hotel. The former, erected by Eastern financier, T. N. McCauley, was ten stories high and was located at Stone and Congress. The twelve-story Pioneer Hotel developed by Harold

Steinfeld opened on December 12, 1929, and quickly became the hub of the central business district as commerce moved north and east from Meyer Street to the hotel's location at Stone and Pennington.[43]

Important as a precursor of Jacome's future participation in international trade was Carlos' departure for Europe shortly after the sale of the "La Bonanza" property. Upon returning, his observations on retailing abroad coupled with his son, Alex's, knowledge of foreign markets gained during a 1927-28 retail sojourn in New York City, probably laid the foundation for Jacome's later participation in international business trade. Leaving on June 25, 1929, with his good friend, cattleman Teofilo Otero, Carlos spent three and one-half months visiting London, Paris, Spain—where he saw the Barcelona Exposition—and Italy. Father Lucas, formerly of the Holy Family Church in Tucson, served as his guide during his stay in Rome. Either he or Bishop Gerke, whom Carlos encountered in Paris on the Bishop's return trip from Rome to Tucson, was responsible for arranging for Carlos a great honor, an audience with the Pope.[44]

Before Carlos left for Europe, Albert Steinfeld returned from New York and gave Tucson's merchants, already harassed by increasing competition, economic news they wanted to hear. According to Steinfeld, business conditions were good. "The reaction from the flurry on the stock market," he stated, had "quieted down and things were now stable."[45] Another economic downturn would have meant bankruptcy for some of Tucson's merchants as they contended with the decreased purchasing power of their customers and growing competition. Reflecting a nationwide trend, customers now had less to spend. This stemmed from their growing habit of spending nearly all they earned and in many cases even more than they earned. The combined effect of more competition for fewer consumer dollars reduced each merchant's share of the total volume of retail sales. Increasingly their behavior was not only defined by internal motivations or by customer expectations but also predicated on the behavior of competitors.[46]

Competition had an especially strong effect on department stores. As chain stores and specialty shops moved into downtown Tucson, Jacome's and Steinfeld's developed a growing interest in their behavior. Chain stores had first come to Tucson in 1913 with S. H. Kress and Company, a variety store chain located in the central business district. As these stores began their extraordinary rate of expansion after the First World War, another variety store, F. W. Woolworth's, located there in 1919. J. C. Penney's, the first chain department store, appeared in 1921, followed by Sears and Montgomery Ward in 1930.[47]

Also during this period, specialty shops and another independent department store appeared in the downtown area to offer competition to Jacome's and Steinfeld's for the next fifty years. One of these specialty shops was Dave Bloom's Men's Wear Store. The Consolidated Bank had called in the lease and loans it held on the Myers and Bloom store in 1930, sold the lease, and gave each of the partners $7,500. At that point, Myers retired, but six months later Bloom opened Dave Bloom's Men's Store.[48] Another specialty shop, Cele Peterson's, grew out of the Co-Ed Shop. Cele Peterson had returned to Tucson to work in her parents' store after attending school in Washington, D.C. and doing research for the Library of Congress in Mexico City. On a bet of $1,000 from two close friends that she would not last more than a month in the "dress business," she took over operation of the shop. During the early years the shop occupied several locations in downtown Tucson, catering to women in Tucson's social set.[49]

The third independent department store coming to downtown Tucson was developed by the Levy family, who bought the Myers and Bloom lease. The Levys had been in retailing since 1902, when they opened the Red Star General Store in Douglas with a $500 investment. Like Jacome's, they had a simple beginning, living in the back of the store, which sat between a saloon and a restaurant. They managed, however, to turn a $7,000 profit the first year.

Changing the store's name to Levy's in 1906, Ben and Jacob Levy incorporated the store as Levy Brothers' Dry Goods Company in 1912, and in 1919 they opened a second store in Douglas called the El Paso Store. The Levy brothers next bought out the Fair Store of Bisbee in 1925. When Jacob's elder son, Aaron, completed his studies at The University of Arizona in 1925, he persuaded his father that "Tucson was the coming hub of southern Arizona and the family business should move there." In 1931 Ben and Jacob took his advice and opened their Tucson store, which featured women's apparel, shoes, housewares, and men's wear.[50]

After 1930, the three department stores, Jacome's Steinfeld's, and Levy's, and specialty shops such as Dave Bloom's and Cele Peterson's shared common problems which characterized the growth of Tucson and change in the down-town business district. Chain store development exacer-bated their problems as Tucson spread and shopping centers grew. Each store developed its own blueprint for survival. Because each made distinctly different decisions about how to survive, they are all extremely relevant to the Jacome story.

Accompanying the growth of retailing units in Tucson was a change in city government. A new city charter was adopted in May of 1929. A result of two years work by an elected twenty-four member board of Tucson's citizens, the charter provided for a city manager and an eight-hour work day for city employees. Another provision, election of councilmen "at large" with nominations made by wards, was criticized by Mexican-Americans who feared their possible disfranchisement by the Anglo majority. Their distrust mirrored their treatment in the community where there was little social interaction between the groups. Anglos and Hispanics sat on different sides of the aisle in St. Augustine Cathedral, and in 1914 the Anglo contingent left to form their own parish. Physicians were required to register a child's ethnicity at birth and were reprimanded if they refused to state "Mexican" on the birth certificate.[51] In public schools, few Mexican-American teachers were employed, and use of Spanish was discouraged. Other differential factors cited in a discrimination suit brought against Tucson Unified School District One in the 1970s were discriminatory teaching assignments for Mexican-American teachers and a transfer policy which allowed Anglo children to leave predominantly Mexican-American schools but limited Mexican-American students' freedom of transfer.[52] What is more, although not legally sanctioned, segregation was a way of life in residential areas.[53]

Economic change was also in the air, whether Tucson's retailers wanted it or not. Albert Steinfeld, on another trip to New York City, had the opportunity to witness the stock market crash and upon returning to Tucson had his observations recorded by the *Tucson Daily Citizen*.

Asserting that the "crash has brought about a situation that is temporary and very temporary at that," he stated his admiration for the "strong hand President Hoover is playing." He then assured Tucson's merchants that he didn't thank "that the financial situation [would] affect Tucson in the least as to business."[54]

Despite Steinfeld's soothing remarks, the Jacome children wanted to take immediate action to cut the store's losses when the crash occurred. Jacome's had thousands of dollars worth of merchandise on order which some of the children thought they should cancel. Carlos refused. "You've made a commitment," he said. "Keep it." They did. This commitment on orders already placed with manufacturers paid off. The Jacomes lost money on the merchandise purchased because they had to sell it at a loss, but they gained several loyal friends among the salesmen and the companies which had received those orders. During World War II when goods became scarce, these same companies saw that Jacome's needs got top priority.[55]

Later, recalling Jacome's experience as the first blows of the Depression hit Tucson, Alex, Sr., found that Jacome's survival was partly attributable to the risk it took in 1925 by moving to the new store location. Apparently the "nest egg rolled up between 1925-1929 helped the store bridge the Depression years."[56] He also stated that

The hard times we went through in the early twen-
ties were a blessing in disguise. . . . We learned
a lesson that was to reap great benefits for us
just a few years later. When the next depression
came we took our losses day by day, marking down
prices on shirts, sheets and socks as the market
declined. As a result, we sold our merchandise and
were able to buy new goods at the lower wholesale
prices that went into effect.

Jacome's went out of its way during the Depression
years to help its customers. During those years many of
the customers could not pay their bills. This was common
and very understandable during a period when many were out
of work and others were living on reduced incomes. Alex
recalled Carlos "talking one day with a woman whose husband
had lost his job." She asked if Jacome's might wait for
payment of their account. "That's what friends are for,"
Carlos said. "Just forget about it until things are better
for you."[57]

The store also gave aid to University of Arizona
professors and district school teachers who were paid in
warrants rather than cash in the early thirties. Jacome's
accepted the warrants, giving each teacher half cash and
half credit to be converted later into cash or merchandise.
Although the common practice was to discount these warrants, Carlos felt the honorable thing to do was to redeem
them at one hundred cents on the dollar.[58] The store's
bookkeeper, Gilbert Martinez, recalled that in those years,
he used far more red ink than black in keeping the company
ledgers.[59]

Carlos explained the renovation of the store which he began in 1931 as a service to the community to help those put on the unemployment roles by the Depression. During the Christmas holidays in 1931, Augustine, the youngest of the Jacome children and a student at St. John's Military Academy in Delafield, Wisconsin, arrived home just in time for the first celebration in the newly expanded store. Jacome's had taken over the second floor, originally occupied by the Savoy Hotel, and more than doubled its original number of square feet of store space, from 7,000 to 15,000. Each department was enlarged, the window display capacity was doubled, and an elevator was installed. Curiously, perhaps because of the Depression, the number of employees had fallen to thirty. Six brothers now worked for the business: Frank, Arthur, Richard, Henry, Ramon, and Alex.[60]

The local contracting firm employed only union labor for the renovation. The store's use of union labor dated back to the early 1920s when during a local labor dispute the Jacomes joined other merchants in posting an "Open Shop" sign in their window. They did this despite the fact that hundreds of their customers, mostly Southern Pacific Railroad employees, were members of a union. When a chain store put up a sign stating, "Friendly to Organized Labor," its sales volume grew impressively. Thereafter, Jacome's made it a point to remind its customers that the store was friendly to organized labor and handled union-made goods. A Labor Day advertisement in 1925 demonstrated that belated enlightenment, reading "Jacome's for Union Made Goods."[61] This new-found sensitivity to customers with union affiliation, however, did not extend to Jacome employees. Enriqueta Martinez DeMeester recalled that Jacome management under pressure gave the employees Saturday afternoon as well as Sunday off from work. Under the guidance of a union organizer, store personnel gathered downtown Saturday afternoon and paraded for the union. When they came to work the following Monday morning, they were told that there would be no more Saturdays off.[62]

After the renovation, Carlos continued to upgrade the store. A few months after the completion of remodeling, he introduced a major technological innovation for Tucson's commercial establishments, an evaporative cooling system. The duct system for the cooler started on the roof of the store, ran to the second and first floors, and then to the basement. It had such force that people could stand in the open front door and get relief from the outdoor heat.[63]

Carlos did not live to see most of the Depression. He died on December 9, 1932, at the age of 62. Dionisia had preceded him, dying suddenly in 1927, and he left the business to his thirteen children. Flags in Tucson flew at half mast and several hundred attended his funeral, held in

St. Augustine Cathedral at 10:00 on a Tuesday morning. Pall-bearers included the prominent businessmen of Tucson: Steinfeld, Drachman, Ronstadt, Carrillo, Felix, Elias, Levy, and Bloom. The sermon was delivered in Spanish. Carlos' last wish was that the store would reopen at 1:00 on Tuesday afternoon. It did.[64]

The Jacome Family, 1890.
Carlos Jacome is fourth from the left.

Interior of Jacome and Manzo Store,
"La Bonanza," 1910

Interior of Jacome Store,
"La Bonanza," 1916

Carlos Jacome and Family

Mrs. Alexander Jacome (Estela Valles), 1934

Alexander Jacome with Salvador Corona (center)

Alexander Jacome

CHAPTER FOUR

TRANSITIONS AND NEW MARKETS

Traditionally, little time is spent on the development of successor regimes in Hispanic organizations,[1] but the centrality of family to the Jacome Department Store had a strong influence on the passage of leadership after Carlos' death. Although different views exist on the amount of influence Mexican-American parents exert over their sons in such matters as educational goals, job expectations, and future plans,[2] Alexander, the tenth of Carlos' and Dionisia's thirteen children, revered his father and from an early age, "shadow[ed] his father's every move," learning the business literally at his father's knee.[3] This knowledge of the business and his college degree in commerce are the reasons usually given for his elevation to the presidency of the store even before Carlos' death.[4]

Was Alex's selection as president simply due to his experience and education, or did he more than the other children exhibit characteristics most like his father's? Some theorists have suggested that executive succession is predicated upon organizational context and that those making the selection tend to favor candidates who are similar to themselves.[5] Thus, did the selection of Alex, especially in view of his number ten position in the family, represent an institutionalization of Carlos' values within the family business?

It is apparent that the close relationship between family and business played an important part in defining the leadership role of father and son. Both subscribed to an authoritarian hierarchical management style and assumed the position as final decision maker. Their tight control of the business was guaranteed through family control of the company. Stock in the firm was a closely held family property passed on to Jacome offspring, with preference given to males. If there were no heirs, it was distributed among the second generation or bought by the corporation. With the latter alternative frequently utilized during Alex's presidency, stock ownership became increasingly consolidated.[6]

Philosophically both Carlos and Alex saw the integrity of the family name as synonymous with the status of the business.[7] Like the Puerto Rican entrepreneur, each regarded the family as a prolongation of his uniqueness, his status in the business world.[8] What combination of Sonoran and frontier Tucson values contributed to this orientation is open to question. Strikingly clear, however, is the precedence family interests took over the maximum exploitation of economic opportunities which characterized twentieth century corporate America. The implications of family priorities for Jacome's business development become clearer as the future of the store unfolds.

Father and son shared other values as well, including a work ethic which emphasized long hours spent on business affairs. They both took a marked interest in the store's customers, spending much of their time "on the floor" although, unlike Carlos, Alex had an office. Personally, they both displayed a strong commitment to the Catholic religion.[9]

There were also definite contrasts between father and son in both background and personality. Whereas Carlos came from a background of poverty and had only three years of formal schooling, Alex had a more affluent upbringing and was the first member of his family to obtain a college degree. With regard to the latter, apparently more than experience and family ties were now necessary in the competitive world of merchandising, with formal credentials and a validation of expertise also becoming essential. This attainment of a college education was exceptional for the time period. Even today, although "a strong value is attached in Hispanic cultures to educating one's children," the percentage completing a college education is small. For example, in 1980, only 9.7 percent of males and 6.2 percent of females of Spanish origin had completed four or more years of college as compared to 17.9 percent of the general population.[10]

Carlos and Alex also possessed decidedly different personalities. Those who knew Carlos described him as "affable, pleasant, well-known and well-liked, polished, and a man who could sell you anything." On the other hand, the terms most often used to describe Alex are "aggressive, hard driving, and achievement oriented."[11] These characteristics are certainly a contrast to two prominent traits typically ascribed to Mexican folk culture: present-time orientation and fatalism. His achievements in high school and throughout life evidenced a mirror image of these folk culture attributes in terms of delayed gratification and the amount of control he perceived over his future.[12] Several examples of his determination to excel came from a classmate at Tucson High School. She remembered his strong desire to become part of the school's debating team. His Spanish accent flavored with a Gallic intonation imparted by French priests at his grammar school, Tucson's Marist College, posed an obstacle to his effectiveness in debate. In fact, his accent inspired much comment from the Mayor's son, provoking Alex to throw a book at him across a classroom.[13]

With the help of the teacher, Alice Vail, he made the debating team and also before graduation nearly walked off with an oratorical prize. Disqualified twice, he staged two comebacks and forged ahead almost to win the state award.[14] Persistence also paid in a state typing contest. One classmate remembers typing much faster than he in class, only to see him win a fifth place at the state meet while she won nothing.[15]

Also unlike Carlos, Alex married outside Tucson's Mexican community. In 1921, Estela Argentina Valles moved to Tucson from Buenos Aires, Argentina, with her physician father, Dr. Fred Valles. Attending a private school in the Tucson area, St. Joseph's Academy, Estela was considered by native Tucsonans as a socially prominent beauty. Alex and she were married on June 17, 1934.[16]

Marriage outside the Mexican community would not dispel the sting of discrimination Alex felt during his youth. Later, comparing his time at The University of Arizona to the social and business world of downtown Tucson, he found fraternities that did not pledge Mexican-Americans and "gringo" girls he could not date. Apparently these actions continued to affect him. Years later when filling out a form for appointment to the Arizona Board of Regents, he volunteered that he was never accepted in a fraternity at the University.[17]

A move to New York City after graduation from the University in 1927 not only gave Alex insight into the positive benefits of his cultural heritage but also broadened his knowledge of retailing. In New York he worked successively for Arnold Constable Company, Gimbel Brothers, and Macy's, where one of his duties was to serve as interpreter for Spanish-speaking customers. Through these contacts he gained a broader vision of commerce and the potential of international trade. He also observed the cultural barriers, including language, that confronted American entrepreneurs who ventured into a Hispanic foreign market. During this period he acquired knowledge of the intricacies of volume buying and selling and other modern merchandising methods. After a brief interlude with the J. C. Penney Company in Laredo, Texas, he returned to Tucson in 1928 to assume the vice presidency of the family store.[18]

From 1929 to 1932, while Alex trained to fill the void which an ailing Carlos would shortly leave in the organization, the Depression was deepening across the nation. By the time Alex assumed the presidency it was apparent to the family that great economic and social change was in the future for Jacome's. Although harbingers of that change had been present in the 1920s, it was in the 1930s that the Jacome family had "to forge a new tradition, one of endurance in adversity."[19]

After approximately 85,000 businesses failed between 1929 and 1932, Franklin Delano Roosevelt took actions to restore the confidence of the nation's businessmen when he assumed office on March 4, 1933. Indeed, when F.D.R. ordered the March 6, 1933, bank holiday to alleviate the critical economic conditions of the Depression, Tucson's businessmen greeted it "in something of a gay spirit."[20] Other legislative measures which followed were similarly perceived, and by the time Alex visited the middle west and east in August and September of 1933, he found "business definitely better" and a great number of unemployed back at work.[21]

Other New Deal actions, however, were measures like the National Industrial Recovery Act (N.I.R.A.) and the Robinson-Patman Act, which would ultimately prove injurious to small independent retailers like Jacome's by contributing to the concentration of the industry. The N.I.R.A., administered through the National Recovery Administration (N.R.A.), combined the interest of business in controlled production; the interest of labor in wages, hours, and collective bargaining; and the interest of many congressmen and presidential advisers in increased spending for public works. Under the law, competing businesses met with governmental, labor, and consumer representatives to draft codes of fair competition which limited production, assigned markets, and established prices.[22]

A major problem with the program which soon became apparent to small businesses like Jacome's was that the N.I.R.A. placed the effective power for code-writing in big business. Consequently, much of the code governing the retailing industry worked to the detriment of small business. Although proclaiming general satisfaction with the

N.R.A., Alex described some of the problems arising from big business control of these codes for the *Tucson Daily Citizen* after his return from a 1933 trip. He found "many manufacturers in many lines who are preparing to take undue advantage of the situation." He also saw some of them already boost[ing] their prices out of all proportion and using the demands of the NRA code to justify the raise.[23]

Declared unconstitutional, the N.I.R.A. was replaced by the Robinson-Patman Act of 1936 which attempted to protect small retailers like Jacome's and ensure them a continuing place in the market. Drafted to eliminate unfair price concessions that large firms enjoyed, this Act also was designed to equalize prices charged by manufacturers for goods purchased directly and indirectly by buyers. The Act explicitly covered brokerage fees and placed a limit on the use of discounts, not through retailers but through wholesalers. A loophole in the Act allowed vendors who sold all their output directly to retailers to grant lower prices than they might ask if using brokers.

Under Robinson-Patman, large firms such as chains with centralized buying procedures could place large volume orders directly with manufacturers, thus gaining "quantity discounts" while avoiding the payment of brokerage fees. Because decentralized buying characterized smaller private firms like Jacome's, a broker was essential, and "quantity discounts" were ruled out. Under the Act several other advantages accrued to large firms. These included support money for advertising and, through the weight of their large orders, the power to discourage suppliers from doing business with smaller competitors.[24]

Another product of Depression-era protectionism, fair trade laws, helped Jacome's to maintain a place in the market by requiring that certain brand-name merchandise carry a fixed price. Federally, these laws stemmed from a 1919 Supreme Court decision which allowed manufacturers to maintain a suggested retail price and the 1937 Miller-Tydings Act which exempted manufacturers from federal anti-trust regulations. Following California's lead in the early 1930s, Arizona passed a fair trade law which con-tained a "nonsigners clause" stipulating that one retail-er's signing of a fair trade agreement bound all other merchants of that branded product in the state to adhere to the manufacturer's minimum resale price. When discount department stores began to appear in Tucson, the local stores used these laws to attack the discounter's low price competitive advantage. Yet, governmental policy during the period had the overall long-range effect of transforming the retail sector at the small retailer's expense.[25]

With such external forces as government regulation adding complexity to the retailing environment, Alex began to change the store's practices during the early years of his presidency. He knew he not only had to accommodate to the shifting Tucson scene but also to the larger national environment. He adopted a merchandise control system which established a balanced relationship between stock and sales in order to yield a larger profit.[26] He also initiated time cards for employees, a payroll system, and expansion of credit through joining a central credit agency. Among other things, Jacome's paid for the first meeting of the Credit Women International in Tucson in 1945.[27]

Advertising took on new forms as well. The store began a "Christmas Club" in which the savers received a 2 percent cash dividend on all purchases.[28] While loyal suppliers maintained the store at the top of their lists for scarce merchandise during World War II, Jacome's emphasized "American-made merchandise."[29] After the war, hosiery houses enabled the store to send out 6,000 pairs of nylons to credit account customers in celebration of the store's fiftieth anniversary in March of 1946. Alex attributed the good will the store generated with different companies during the Great Depression "as the reason why eight major stock producers and their salesmen got [Jacome's] that supply during this period of nylon shortage."[30]

Probably from the year spent outside Tucson, Alex realized that to increase the store's volume, which was $300,000 annually in 1932, he would have to broaden his span of contacts, both within retailing and throughout the broader customer community. One of his first moves was to become a member of the Board of Directors of the Western States Merchants' Association in 1933. This was an association which met semi-annually to view new merchandise displayed and sold by Western manufacturers and wholesalers. The purpose of the organization was to develop the retail and wholesale trade in the Western states with the intent of keeping business in their own region.[31]

Because of the Depression and the resulting unemployment, however, the number of Mexican-American customers was not growing. As the *Arizona Daily Star* reported in September of 1932, the unemployment rate for Tucson had grown to 4,000 persons. Racial tensions over jobs were exacerbated by the increasing unemployment and were beginning to resemble those encountered by Carlos during the 1893 depression.[32] Of course, the early summer encampment of a large contingent of the Bonus Army showed that much of the economic strife was divorced from racial conflict. This group, composed of First World War veterans on their way to Washington, D.C., to lobby Congress for immediate issuance of bonuses not due them until 1945, rolled into Tucson during the month of June in a large fleet of old automobiles. After one day and one night, Tucson was looking forward with pleasure to its departure.[33]

Yet, as unemployment soared, racism played a major role as American citizens of Mexican descent as well as

Mexican nationals became targets for deportation. Some
left voluntarily, encouraged by local governments or private agencies, because they could no longer find jobs.
Others left through forced repatriation. Indigent Mexican-
Americans not wanting to leave were loaded on buses,
trains, and trucks and sent to Mexico because they were
unemployed or seemed likely to become unemployed. Governmental regulations actually supported these actions, defining Mexicans as "probably foreign." Agencies placed the
burden of proof of citizenship on the individual rather
than the government.[34] Deportation was accompanied by a
significant reversal of immigration from Mexico after 1930,
even though United States immigration laws were not
changed. Reinterpretation of existing laws made immigration from Mexico legally very difficult. Two principal
instruments for legally restricting immigration were the
contract labor provision and the literacy test. The former, passed in 1885 at the request of organized labor, was
originally designed as "a blanket prohibition of employers
from recruiting labor in Europe and paying for their passage across the Atlantic." Now it was simply extended to
Mexican nationals. A third method was denial of entry to
anyone "likely to become a public charge." The vagueness
of this restriction left a great deal to the investigator's
discretion. For instance, if an applicant claimed he had
"a job waiting in the United States," denial was based on

the contract labor provision. If the applicant admitted no job existed, rejection was based on prospective indigent status.[35]

Faced with declining Mexican-American clientele, Alex turned to a growing market sixty-five miles from Tucson: Mexico. "Figuring it one good business if we could get it," Alex and his brothers traveled over the dusty, bumpy roads of northern Mexico making contacts during the 1930s and 1940s. Later these contacts extended all the way to Mexico City. Out of these first contacts came a growing number of customers, not only for Jacome's but also for the other retailers in the downtown shopping area. According to specialty shop owner, Cele Peterson, "If Alex had not wined and dined the Mexicans that trade would never have materialized." And what a trade it turned out to be! In December of 1957 alone, 1,500 shoppers from the single state of Sonora would come north to Tucson to do their Christmas shopping.[36]

Alex's campaign "to break down the distrust the people of Mexico had for the 'gringos' to the north"[37] reached far beyond simply wining and dining the customers. He carried on a large correspondence with contacts in Mexico and arranged to help people in such diverse ways as getting students into the University and setting up accounts for them to draw upon,[38] assisting the sick seeking hospitalization, or getting them out of jail in the middle

of the night and finding them a hotel room.[39] This service
for Tucson's Mexican neighbors was conducted by Jacome's on
a round-the-clock basis. It was not unusual for a Mexican
tourist--out of gasoline and out of dollars--to phone Alex
or one of his brothers in the middle of the night from a
country service station. Explaining that the gas station
operator would not accept his pesos in payment for gasoline, the tourist would arrange for Alex to send dollars to
cover the purchase with repayment in pesos to be made
later. Alex generated further good will by prevailing upon
Tucson's doctors to go into Mexico on public health mis-
sions and agricultural specialists at the University to
journey south to give advice on control of crops or insect
problems.[40]

One of the first times Alex had an opportunity to
aid a Mexican citizen was in the early 1930s when a former
revolutionary leader, General Anselmo Macias, then Governor
of Sonora, was suffering from an impacted tooth and needed
a dentist. The General was not amenable to leaving his
pistol behind when he crossed the border into the United
States although U.S. law required him to do so. He phoned
Alex, who came to the border and obtained permission for
the General to retain his weapon during his stay in
Arizona. Then the General would not allow the Tucson
dentist to perform the necessary surgery unless Alex was in
the operating room with him. So Alex donned a white

surgical mask and stood beside the General, who still had his .45 calibre pistol strapped to his waist, while the surgery was performed. The entire dental operation was performed satisfactorily with Macias, a man with an obviously suspicious nature, refusing to be "put to sleep" during the proceeding. When the operation was over, the General and his five aides retired to the General's hotel suite with a case of Scotch and played poker for three days while the General recuperated.[41]

The Jacome name became so well-known in Mexico that one day Manuel Corella, who lived in a small town in the mountains of Sonora, included the Tucson store in his marriage plans. Manuel and his fiancee, an American citizen, had been separated for some time. Through many letters to her in Los Angeles, he finally convinced her that they should marry. They agreed to meet at Jacome's. At 9:00 on the appointed morning, a Saturday, Alex arrived at the store and discovered Manuel pacing back and forth outside. He had been there since 7:30. When his betrothed finally arrived, it became apparent that there were no arrangements for the wedding. Manuel did not know where to get the license, where to find the local priest, or where to get flowers for his bride. Jacome's took care of these things for Manuel and even negotiated a special dispensation for them to marry the following day. Employees from Jacome's served as the couple's attendants.[42]

On another occasion a woman from Mexico City called
Alex at the store, saying that she was not well and that
she hoped he could help. Arranging an appointment for her
with a Spanish-speaking doctor, Alex later learned that the
woman had returned to Mexico City after a rapid recovery.
He met her there a year later and found her to be the
glowing picture of health. She took Jacome aside and
revealed the diagnosis prescribed by his Tucson doctor, "My
husband used to tell me had to go off on business trips,"
she said. "Only I learned he wasn't working. He was
seeing other girls. I was so unhappy my health became poor
until I saw your doctor in Tucson. He told me the next
time my husband went off like that, I should disappear for
a few days." So she did. Not bothering to tell her husband, she left to visit relatives in Guanajuato. Upon her
return, a loving husband renounced his business trips.
According to the woman, "none of the doctors in Mexico City
would give me advice like that--because they all play golf
with my husband."[43]

Another good will gesture which made Jacome's so
popular with Mexican tourists was the store's willingness
to accept the Mexican peso on the same basis as United
States currency. It was the first Tucson store to do so.
Even though the Tucson Trade Bureau urged other downtown
stores to follow Jacome's lead, several refused. The store
gave the Mexican customer even exchange at a slightly

better rate than the bank. According to Alex, "he didn't fuss with [the] decimal point. . . . Why worry about that chicken feed. It builds good will and that's worth far more than we lose on the exchange." Anyone returning to Mexico with excess dollars could trade his accumulated dollars for pesos with the store. If the store retained an overly large number of pesos, Alex could take them to the Southern Arizona Bank for a trade. According to his banker, the major risk Alex took in accepting pesos was deflation, but to his knowledge, Jacome's "was never caught."[44]

Future statistics would reveal the amount of trade engendered by this practice of peso exchange. In 1958, for example, the store exchanged three and one-half million pesos--roughly $200,000 in U.S. currency. Not all of this was spent at Jacome's, but the store accommodated its Mexican guests regardless of what they planned to do with their money. Peso exchange was also accompanied by credit extended to Jacome's Mexican customers. Using his contacts south of the border, Alex personally investigated the backgrounds of those applying for credit with the help of his credit manager, Enriqueta DeMeester. It was a procedure that grew easier as the years passed. The manager of Steinfeld's, Jim Davis, remembers visiting Hermosillo with Alex for a trade seminar, both growing tired of the meetings and leaving to visit the city. Everywhere they went it seemed "people knew Alex and he knew everyone."[45]

In many different ways the Jacomes emphasized their contacts with Mexico. In 1939, the store had a promotional contest for the oldest pair of shoes in Tucson. In their window they displayed old shoes from several different countries. The shoes from old Mexico were considered the most elegant of all. As described in the *Arizona Daily Star*, "Seventy-three years ago a senorita danced in lavender satin shoes with tassel bows and beaded applique. Boots of the same year are lavish with gilt and beads. And even baby's shoes had gay little bows lined with gilt and tiny flat heels."[46]

On September 11, 1941, a *Tucson Daily Citizen* editorial hailed Alex as "A Worthy Ambassador" to the second Pan-American Highway Congress convened in Mexico City to open "freer communications between the republics of the Western hemisphere as facilitated by travel." Noting that he was representing the Tucson Chamber of Commerce and acting as personal representative of Governor Osborn, the *Citizen* maintained that in a "wider sense he also represent[ed] the Southwest which is bound to the Latin sisters by ties of blood and race" and that Alex's "kindness and understanding personified the North American attitude toward the Pan American countries under President Roosevelt." The *Citizen* also projected its future expectations of Alex's diplomatic opportunities. With almost uncanny accuracy, the paper predicted that "the time must surely come when from the Hispaniolated Southwest such men will be recruited by the State Department to exemplify the fused identity of Pan America and instrument the diplomatic liaison between north and south."[47]

As "Tucson Rotary's first native son president," Alex continued his career as good will ambassador and Pan-American diplomat when he was able to arrange, "after working toward it for eighteen years," a meeting between the Tucson Rotary Club and the Magdalena, Sonora, Mexico Rotarians. These meetings would become a tradition between the two clubs. At the first meeting the Sonoran guests were paired with Tucson Rotarians like Dave Bloom of Dave Bloom and Son's to see how their Tucson counterparts conducted their day-to-day business. According to Alex, they could "thus understand our actions and thoughts better . . . promoting understanding between the two nations." On May 5, 1946, Alex led Tucson Rotarians across the border for a visit with the Magdalena Rotarians and to celebrate the Fifth of May, one of Mexico's important holidays. This Pan-American good will promotion continued in 1947, when Alex took part in an Arizona trade committee meeting with a similar committee in Sonora, Mexico, to develop plans for trade between the two areas.[48]

Hermosillo, Sonora, Mexico, also had a special reason, which dated back to the days of World War II, for regarding Alex as a good will ambassador. During that conflict, diesel oil was scarce, and at one point a shipment went astray, leaving Hermosillo with only a three-day supply. As Jacome family friend and manager of the electric generating plant, Don Ramon Corral, told Alex, a tanker was bringing a supply from Tampico but would not arrive for at least two or three weeks. Alex telephoned a Tucson oil dealer and told him, "They need twenty carloads" of oil in Hermosillo. The dealer said, "There's a war on." Alex replied, "Get on the phone and charge it to me." Through the help of Arizona Senator Carl Hayden and the Ambassador to Mexico, he was able to get export permits for the diesel. From various refineries in California and elsewhere, he rounded up twenty carloads of diesel, and within four days it was on its way to Hermosillo. Probably due to fuel rationing in the United States, which grew in severity as the war years progressed, this heroic mission was not given local publicity. A few days later, the Hermosillo newspaper, *El Imparcial*, however, ran a headline, "Jacome Saves Lights of Hermosillo."[49]

During the Second World War a common complaint in Tucson among the Mexican-American population was that "too many men of Mexican ancestry were inducted into the armed services in Tucson . . . more than the Mexican ratio in the community population would warrant."[50] Certainly the Jacome family contributed its share to the war effort. The store was the first in Tucson to answer the plea for financing the war with a $20,000 subscription. Also, Henry and Augustine served in the army and Arthur in the navy. Henry hoped to see some of the action he missed during World War I when his army unit, assigned to France, got as far as Benson, Arizona, before the armistice was declared, but he spent the second war in Salina, Kansas. Getting some of the action Henry missed, Augustine was issued an army parka and winter underwear and then was sent to the Mariana Islands in the South Pacific [sic]. The naval vessel to which Arthur was assigned was torpedoed, and he spent several days in the ocean before being rescued.[51]

With several of the family members gone, Alex, Richard, and the twins were left to run the store. Spurred by Alex, Jacome's employees sold five times more war bonds than all other Tucson department stores together. During the war years Jacome's also began a scholarship for merchandising students at The University of Arizona in memory of Carlos and Dionisia. They supplemented that donation in 1945 with a U.A. Memorial of $2,600 for a room in the Student Union.[52]

During the 1930s and through the war years until the move to Stone and Pennington, Alex continued to share an office with Jacome's credit manager. He also continued to work with the firms and the salesmen with whom his father had established relationships. Like Carlos, he frequently brought them home for dinner.[53] A June 10, 1940, photo in the *Tucson Daily Citizen* shows Alex receiving a silver medal and congratulations from the salesman of one of these old firms, Walk-Over Shoes, to mark the thirtieth anniversary of that firm's relationship with the store.[54]

The store had expanded in 1937 before the war[55] and in 1946 with the end of the war came another expansion. Along with the post-war expansion went a complete redecoration. The store now had murals painted by well-known Mexican artist, Salvador Corona, decorating the walls. A former bull fighter, Corona met Alex in 1940 at a Rotary Club supper in Nogales, Sonora. Years later he recalled Alex's many kindnesses to him, especially when he broke his hip and was taken to the hospital. Alex picked him up at the hospital and took him home saying, "Salvador, ask me whatever you want or need and I'll give it to you."[56] When the store reopened on March 16, 1946, in celebration of its fiftieth anniversary, customers were rewarded not only with the chance to view Corona's murals but also a picture of Carlos on the balcony.[57]

Like Jacome's, which now had one hundred employees and a $100,000 inventory,[58] the other retail establishments in downtown Tucson were undergoing change. Steinfeld's expanded their store in 1933 and celebrated an eightieth birthday in 1935, the same year Albert died, leaving management of the firm to his son, Harold.[59] The co-founders of Levy's, Ben and Jacob, parted company in 1935. Jacob retained the Tucson store while Ben took the Douglas and Bisbee stores. Ben died in 1945, Jacob in 1946. Jacob's sons, Aaron and Leon took over management of the Tucson store.[60] Opened in 1931, Dave Bloom's Men's Store was incorporated in 1940 and renamed Dave Bloom and Sons.[61] In 1949, Levy's announced the development of a new two and one-half story store with a basement to be built at Scott and Pennington.[62]

Whether journeying from Mexico or from Tucson's suburbs, Jacome's shoppers increasingly found transportation systems to accommodate them. Although the Depression reduced the number of trains arriving in Tucson daily from five to three, the Second World War increased railroad passenger traffic to its peak of six arrivals per day. Passenger volume on Tucson's motor buses during the Second World War increased over 550 percent, while there was a 400 percent increase in the size of the transit fleet.[63] At the same time, the increasing use of automobiles brought plans to install parking meters downtown.[64] Jacome's and other retailers were beginning to realize the parking problems inherent in the increased use of the automobile. Traffic flow into and out of downtown on streets built for an earlier era was also an increasing problem. Yet, the growing use of the automobile had its advantages. Now merchants could court customers outside the community, not only in Mexico but in other southern Arizona towns.[65] In 1948, Tucson's retail trading area had grown to encompass Nogales, 65 miles from Tucson, with a population of 7,000; Bisbee, 100 miles away, with a population of 6,000; Douglas, 125 miles away, with a population of 10,000; and Safford, 137 miles from Tucson, with a population of 5,000.[66]

Also contributing to the growth of customers and profits were the development of natural resources, the growth of local markets, and increasing capital. All of these were making Tucson into an industrial urban society.[67] Jacome's had increased its net profits during the war. But the increase was less than during the First World War because of taxation, greater social expenses, and stipulations covering the control of prices and markups. After the war, due to the large volume of unsatisfied demand for all kinds of goods and backed by a great accumulated reserve of purchasing power, the growing Tucson population helped them to enjoy a continuous increase in their profit margins.[68]

Other independent department stores across the country were reaping similar rewards after the war, but change was in the air. Two forms of retail trade, the department store chain and the national holding company were beginning to achieve new levels of growth.[69] The Depression of the 1930s had played a significant role in the rise of the chain store. Lagging sales and declining profit rates increased centralization of supervision and control. Stores like J. C. Penney's and Sears became pioneers in development of electronic inventory systems and the use of the full range of media for advertising. Retail holding companies of wholly owned, geographically dispersed firms, each maintaining its customer identity and local management, were benefiting from many of the same factors favorable to chains. Like the chains, they were able to take advantage of cooperative advertising and centralized allocation of resources. A third innovation in the retailing field, the discount department store, first appeared in Massachusetts in 1948. But that apparently posed no immediate threat to the full service independents like Jacome's and Steinfeld's nor to chains and holding company acquisitions.[70] Geographically isolated from the mainstream of American commercial life and still insulated from the growing complexity of retailing nationwide, Tucson's retailers looked forward to the 1950s with optimism.

CHAPTER FIVE

THE MILLION DOLLAR STORE

"This is new in Tucson," announced *The Wall Street Journal* on August 21, 1950. "Maybe Macy's doesn't tell Gimbel's but Steinfeld builds for Jacome."[1] A week later, *Time* magazine elaborated: "In Tucson, Arizona . . . the names Steinfeld's and Jacome's are like Macy's and Gimbel's in Manhattan . . . and they are red-hot competitors." Yet, the $1,000,000 store which Jacome's was building across the street from Steinfeld's would be built by "none other than arch-competitor Steinfeld's which owns the property, and will lease the new building to Jacome." The presidents of the two firms gave individual assessments of the project with Alex declaring "he was getting one of the best sites in town," while Harold Steinfeld asserted it "should set a new high standard of clean unselfish business competition."[2]

So Jacome's and Steinfeld's together with the other retailers in downtown Tucson began the era of the 1950s, one of the longest, steadiest periods of growth and prosperity in American history. Growth during this period was due to many factors, including credit expansion and population growth. In fact, across the United Stated during the era an explosion in credit fueled retail development. In

100

1950, for example, the ratio of credit to disposable income was 10.4 percent with 21.5 billion worth of debt outstanding. Only a decade later, the ratio to disposable income had grown to 16.1 percent, and the total debt outstanding stood at 56.1 billion.[3] Within this ten-year span, two recessions did occur, one in 1954-55 and another in 1957-58, but consumer spending remained stable.[4]

As migration to the Sunbelt expanded, Tucson's population grew right along with Jacome's. And although the downtown retailer held supremacy, on the outskirts of town shopping centers were appearing: Swanway, 1954; Country Fair, 1956; Southgate, 1957; Casas Adobes Center, 1957; Amphi Plaza, 1958; and Monterey Village, 1958.[5] As new subdivisions opened on the east side of town, which the City annexed almost as quickly as they developed, Speedway, Broadway, and Twenty-Second Street became the main arteries to reach them.[6]

The story behind the new Jacome store at Stone and Pennington, which became a reality in 1951, was more involved than *Women's Wear Daily*, *The Wall Street Journal*, *Time*, or other national publications conveyed.[7] In Alex's words, "After the war years, it became apparent that our store was too small . . . if we were to continue our expansion and growth. I knew that this meant a move since the present store at Congress and Scott could not be enlarged, so I looked around and one night lying awake an idea was

born--why not next to a competitor?"[8] The Sunday morning
golf game he played with Harold Steinfeld at the Tucson
Country Club after Mass took on an added meaning. With a
five-stroke handicap because he played "exuberantly," but
with little skill,[9] Alex negotiated with Harold through the
nine holes they habitually played and the breakfast of eggs
and jalapenas which followed.[10] This continued for three
years, with the bargaining focused on the site at the
corner of Stone and Pennington where the Steinfeld grocery
and lunch counter had stood for more than thirty years and
also on the adjoining property, the former home of the
Tucson Gas, Electric Light, and Power Company. After more
than a year, Harold agreed to a one-story building.
Another year yielded a second story. When finally built,
the store had three levels, two above ground and one below,
with a foundation which would support an additional fourth
level.[11]

One clause of the thirty-year lease completing the
deal held future ramifications for Jacome's. This clause
specified that Jacome's would not put up another store
within fifteen miles of downtown.[12] Harold's nephew, Jim
Davis, later recalled he thought the most detrimental
portion of the lease was the limitation placed on Jacome's
mobility. According to Davis, "his uncle owned so much
property downtown, he couldn't see anything beyond the
downtown underpass." This was the conclusion others drew

as well. A wholesaler commented that "Mr. Steinfeld is making a very wise move for his own interest. He is concentrating business in a district where his store is" located.[13]

It took approximately a year of work by an average of twenty workmen putting in 29,000 hours of labor to erect the store. This included the time necessary to demolish the buildings which formerly occupied the site. The M. M. Sundt Construction Company was in charge of construction, and Tucson architect, Terry Atkinson, designed the building. With approximately three times the selling space of the old store at Congress and Scott, the store was 100 feet wide fronting on Stone Avenue and 145 feet deep along Pennington Street, with major entrances on both streets. The only windows in the building were for display purposes, those running the full length of the front and side. The Jacome family installed the latest technological advances, including year-round air conditioning, fluorescent flood-lighting and incandescent spotlighting throughout the store, a sprinkler system for fire protection, and two passenger elevators. There were also customer conveniences which the company had been unable to provide at Congress and Scott: four restrooms and lounges, a playroom for children, and a large parking lot which would hold one hundred and fifty cars.[14]

Both the interior and exterior of the store reflected the influence of earlier Southwestern buildings. Within the store, desert-toned hues and Indian and Mexican motifs, designed and produced exclusively for Jacome's by artists Dale Nichols and Salvador Corona, predominated. Nichols completed three murals on the east side of the second level showing a typical Mexican village, a family group, and a fiesta scene. Corona had eight murals on the first floor, the same murals which he had originally done for Jacome's old store at Scott and Congress in 1946. Edith Hamlin Dale designed two huge identical panels to go over the Stone Avenue and Pennington Street doors. Although not completed in time for the opening, the panels, ten by eleven feet in size and weighing more than 1,500 pounds each, depicted Spanish Franciscan Fray Marcos de Niza on an exploration trip to Arizona.[15]

Pre-opening tension was heightened when a fire broke out in the store's interior forty-eight hours before the planned celebration. Exhausted from sleepless nights of worrying about finances and the opening, Alex, Sr., had gone to bed early only to be aroused at 2:00 in the morning by the Tucson Fire Department. Heart pounding, he rushed to the store where he was met by three fire engines. There he viewed the ruins of still smoldering carpet scraps on the second floor which a careless carpet layer had ignited with a misplaced cigarette. The new sprinkler system had proved an effective fire protection device, but a pungent odor filled the store. Employees bought deodorizers and placed them in every room, and plans continued apace for the target date, September 11, 1951.[16]

The Grand Opening had "all the pomp of a religious pageant and the gaiety of a Mexican fiesta."[17] It also reflected that identity with culture, the friendliness, and the feeling of community which characterized Jacome's throughout its existence. Streets in front and beside the building were roped off to accommodate the crowds. Music by a ten-piece Mexican orchestra, singing by Los Carlistas, and the Tucson Boys' Chorus provided entertainment. Among the honored guests were Arizona Governor Howard Pyle, Sonoran Governor Ignacio Soto, Tucson Mayor Fred Emery, and the Mayor of Ures, Sonora. One hundred old-time customers of Jacome's were special guests. Also present were representatives of Tucson's ethnic and religious groups: Frank Wong, president of the Chinese Chamber of Commerce; Thomas Segundo, chief of the Papago Tribal Council; Morgan Maxwell, principal of Spring Elementary School; Albert Bilgray, president of the Synagogue Council; and Harold L. Langer, president of the Tucson Ministers' Association. Barry Goldwater, then president of Goldwater's Department Store in Phoenix, also numbered among the honored.[18]

Highlighting the decorations was a large banner stretched across Stone Avenue between Jacome's and

Steinfeld's which showed the clasp of two hands. A picture of this was carried by the wire service to newspapers throughout the nation and was also featured in national magazines. In keeping with the fiesta spirit, Alex had made in Mexico a very large pinata, a seven-foot clown filled with candies, pennies, nickels, and dimes. With ten smaller pinatas in various animal shapes and containing candy, gum, favors, and small gift certificates, Alex provided a special party for children from six to ten years old.[19]

The official festivities began with a group of mariachis playing to keep the spirit going as more than 20,000 persons gathered. Promptly at 6:30 p.m., the ringing of cathedral bells was followed by the Tucson Boys' Chorus singing Gounod's "Ave Maria." As the first notes sounded, his Excellency Bishop Daniel J. Gercke emerged from the Pioneer Hotel and crossed the street accompanied by Monsignor Green and Monsignor Gramer. Attired in colorful robes, they entered the new store, stopping at the entrance to begin ancient ceremonial rites to bless the structure. Frequently seen in Latin countries, this ritual was practically never used in the United States in connection with a commercial structure. They then proceeded through the store, blessing the foundation, merchandise, and fixtures. Following several short speeches, the doors were thrown open and the crowds flowed through all three

floors.   Alex felt "a warm feeling glow[ing] within me, to
see so many people viewing the store.   It was then I knew
that Jacome's had real friends."   The following day, the
Citizen carried a public letter from Harold Steinfeld.   It
read in part:

> You and I are fortunate to have been born and
> raised in Tucson and to have had the opportunity of
> witnessing its remarkable growth far beyond the
> fondest expectations of our fathers.   I congratu-
> late you for the prominent part you have taken in
> this development.[20]

Suppliers from throughout the United States re-
sponded to the publicity on the Jacome-Steinfeld deal as
well as on the store opening.   Long-time associates like
Society Brand Clothes, John B. Stetson Company, and Walk-
Over Shoes vied with other wholesalers for Jacome's business.   Alemany and Erlman, Inc., petitioned Jacome's to
incorporate Salvador Dali ornaments into their jewelry
department while Morgan Jones, Inc., suggested that the
store carry its brand of bedspreads and draperies.[21]

After moving into the new store, Jacome employees,
now numbering almost two hundred,[22] for the first time had
their own room where they could "rest, eat lunch and brew a
little coffee."   Such a room in any organization can serve
the purpose of unifying employees or as a gathering place
for dissenters.   In this case it was the former.   One
employee noted that although some using the room "tended to
cheat on the ten cents required for a cup of coffee, they
always kept the room nice and clean."[23]   Such care

indicated the employees' respect for a room not "owned" by anyone where they could meet informally. Apparently with the store assuming much larger proportions, management understood the importance of this central gathering place. Here individual members of the growing work force avoided potential isolation within the store while the integral culture, so important to any organization, was maintained.[24]

Alex also benefited from the move, gaining a large private office of his own for the first time. This was out of the flow of the store and he rarely used it. Preferring to sit at a desk in front of the office employees, Alex primarily used the office, known as the "crying room" among store personnel, for discipline purposes, and to meet with close associates like Gilbert Martinez and Richard Jacome for strategy planning sessions. There he also entertained out-of-town guests and well-known personalities. For example, in November of 1954, he probably met there with Faustino Felix, President of Cuidad Obregon, Mexico. As Alex explained to Tucson Mayor Fred Emery, a group of Tucson's citizens would meet at Jacome's to accompany Faustino on his tour of Tucson's public works.[25]

Besides this luxurious office and private bathroom, Alex was departing from the lifestyle established by Carlos in other ways. He now held membership in prestigious organizations like the Tucson Country Club and the Old

Pueblo Club. In March of 1957, he moved to the exclusive upper-class residential area, El Encanto, which had one "Spanish" family in 1950.[26] Tucsonans interviewed in 1961 about power and status in the City agreed that the most important class determinants for Mexican-Americans were occupation, income (wealth), and family line. They also indicated that wealthy businessmen from pioneer families were eligible for upper-class status and that "the family which owned the department store . . . belonged to the [Mexican-American] upper class and to that of the greater community as well."[27]

Yet an ambivalent attitude existed in the Mexican-American community toward those of their culture who attained status as members of the community elite. A majority of respondents to the 1961 survey indicated that these men identified themselves so completely socially and culturally with the dominant Anglo group that they no longer considered themselves "Mexican." Yet these respondents also looked up to these men. One person interviewed offered an explanation for this ambivalence. After criticizing prominent Mexican-Americans for having become "Anglicized," this respondent maintained, "The only way to get ahead in this town is to get in with the 'American' [Anglo] big shots. That's where all the money is."[28]

Alex numbered among the elite at a time when the first "American of Mexican descent" in the twentieth century, Robert Salvatierra, was elected to the Tucson school board in a campaign marked with ugly racial and religious overtones.[29] Also, although Tucson ranked "high" in its level of residential segregation,[30] Alex moved into a prestigious upper-class Anglo neighborhood. Apparently his ability to gain acceptance by the Anglo leadership was predicated both on his success in business and his involvement, even more than Carlos', in the mainstream of community affairs. An authority on Hispanic business practices has noted that "historically, philosophically, and logically, the business enterprise system appears to present the greatest opportunity for facilitating mainstreaming of Hispanics into the Anglo world." Maintaining that mainstreaming can occur "without the abandonment of Hispanic social and cultural characteristics," this observer sees "mainstreaming as distinct from assimilation, which implies the loss of unique social and cultural characteristics." Mainstreaming "permits a full participation in majority activities and allows free access to positions of power and influence within the majority."[31]

By the time of his death, Alex's mainstreaming activities included membership on the Arizona Board of Regents, the Rotary Club, the Tucson Airport Authority, the Pima County Hospital Advisory Committee, the Tucson Metropolitan Chamber of Commerce, the Tucson Merchant's Association, the Sunshine Climate Club, Elks, and the Newcomen

Society. He also served as honorary Vice-Consul of Mexico and participated in numerous other groups which enhanced his reputation both locally and nationally. In 1948, for instance, the *Arizona Daily Star* reported that he was on the board of directors that set up the Tucson Medical Center when it became a community hospital. In 1954, he was named to a special board to study the minimum wage for women and minors in the retail trade industry.[32]

An important component of these activities was his work on U.S. delegations in hemispheric and European economic and social relations. In August of 1954, he headed a five-man delegation from the United States to the Third Inter-American Indian Congress held at La Paz, Bolivia. At this conference, he spent a month discussing the problems of health, education, and general welfare among the Indians of Latin America.[33] Finding that 50 percent of the population of Latin America was Indian and 90 percent was illiterate, he suggested "that the Indians be taught their own language first then Spanish," a curious perception when compared with his later comments on bilingual education.[34] Appointed by Secretary of State John Foster Dulles in 1955 to a six-year term as the official U.S. representative to the Inter-American Indian Institute headquartered in Mexico City, Alex was elected chairman of the executive committee in 1956.[35] By 1957, Senator Barry Goldwater of Arizona was defining Alex as "one of the outstanding experts" in the United States on the affairs of Latin America.[36]

In 1959, his involvement in international relations broadened to include Spain when he was appointed as a member of a trade mission to that country by the Bureau of Commerce. Specifically organized to stimulate tourist development in Spain as well as to assess that country's trade potential with the United States, the Commission profited both from Alex's advice on manufactured goods and his linguistic ability. He used the latter frequently to address "prominent officers, governors, mayors and an enormous number of business leaders." According to Alex's son, Alex F. Jacome, Jr., his father's Spanish colleagues joked with him about his Mexican accent. And after his return from Spain, Alex received a cartoon from a Spanish acquaintance lightly "poking fun" at his particular use of Spanish idioms. This cartoon became the store's 1959 Christmas card.[37]

While in Spain Alex found "a great many products . . . he believed would find a strong market in Arizona."[38] For several years he had nurtured the idea of importing Spanish furniture for the store,[39] and with this official visit, his dream became reality. He brought several pieces back to Tucson to see whether they would sell. The success of that exploratory venture led Jacome's into the import business by 1960.[40]

Although modest in assessing her contributions to the firm, Estela Jacome was an important element in the success of the Spanish import business as well as the more general growth of the store. Her role was consistent with the family nature of many Hispanic businesses, where women play a large and pivotal role.[41] It also fit with the traditional role assigned to wives of high-ranking officials in American corporate life; they projected the top manager's private persona for public inspection while carrying out a multitude of diplomatic duties. Although Estela regarded the business as a "one man show,"[42] she was essential in entertaining at home, at social affairs, and in business entertainment. Locally, nationally, and internationally, Estela assumed the role of official hostess and public relations professional when Jacome's sought "legitimacy and support from those important groups in the external environment whether suppliers, governmental agencies, political groups or customers."[43] No area of her life remained untouched by responsibility for the company. Upon Alex's appointment in 1954 as a delegate to the Inter-American Indian Congress, Estela left her summer vacation home in La Jolla, California, and "all in one week . . . rushed home, put away my summer clothes, got all my winter clothes out of storage and arranged for the children's care. . . . I barely made the plane."[44]

Estela first became involved with Jacome's Spanish imports because of her knowledge of lace used in Spanish mantillas. Because of her excellent language skills and cultural background as well as her considerable personal charm, the involvement grew. This was especially the case when it was found that Spanish merchants would bring items for her inspection which they would not show commercially to others. Progressively, her buying trips with Alex led away from Madrid and Barcelona along endless dirt roads to tiny villages. There they spent long hours bargaining with owners of small furniture factories. Estela's description of a visit to the village of San Seca, Spain, is typical of these trips. It began with a long drive to the village where the furniture factory was found behind the owner's home. The owner and workmen greeted them upon arrival with wine and music and several hours of socializing; they then settled down to business.[45]

Back in Tucson, Estela trained the store's clerks, such as import shop department head, Grace Bourguignon, on how to present the articles for sale. Rather than preparing them for a high-pressured sales pitch, Estela emphasized knowledge of the products. This practice of individualized personalized training of all Jacome sales staff continued to dominate at the store. Especially noteworthy because nationwide chain stores had begun to minimize the product knowledge of sales people, this practice also diverged from the chains' growing focus upon the almost mechanical use of sales people as order takers and processors of commodities.

According to Grace, "Shortly after each trip to Spain, Estela arrived at the store, beautifully groomed," and over lunch they discussed the various pieces purchased, their background and significance. Years later, Grace still conveyed the love and appreciation she had for the art and furniture displayed in her department. She described in detail the hand-rubbed walnut furniture, kiln dried to protect it from Arizona's arid climate, and other articles in the shop, including hand-forged wrought iron crosses. Several celebrities patronized the shop, but the one Grace remembered most clearly was radio commentator Paul Harvey, who bought one of her favorite pieces. One day he admired an imported Spanish statue made of 1,200-year-old olive wood, and "at the last minute before he was about to walk out the door, decided to buy it [and] . . . wouldn't even let me wrap it up."[46]

Estela and Grace's relationship symbolized a continuation of the esprit de corps Carlos established at Jacome's between personnel and management. It rested upon a personalized environment with the employees having a tacit though positive identification with the store itself or with its owners. As a former employee wrote to Alex in 1950, "Ever since I was associated with your store as a saleslady . . . I have had a warm spot in my heart for it and for all of you who were so kind and friendly to me."[47] In interviews, former store employees with long service at the store cited "being part of the family" as a major factor in their tenure. Informal activities like the get-togethers outside the store which were so popular during the years of Carlos' management continued to generate this feeling of "family" among store personnel. Formal meetings also established the employee's value to the store. Jacome's management encouraged employees to attend a meeting each Saturday to discuss the way business was going and to suggest new approaches to merchandising. Alex's favorite saying at these meetings was that "three heads are better than one;" but as one employee noted, "he already had his own thoughts on the matter, but was a very good diplomat."[48]

Another factor contributing to employees' perceptions of a collective spirit at Jacome's was the concern management showed for their personal well being. When Toleta Martinez's husband became very ill, she requested a part-time job to replace the full-time one she held so she could care for him. Augustine Jacome suggested she remain full-time and work only the days and hours she could. For several months, she worked part-time for a full-time salary.[49] Grace Bourguignon remembered the day she was running out the door for lunch with her glasses slipping off her nose. Alex, Sr., grabbed her hand, gave her some money, and said, "You go and get new glasses."[50] Management also emphasized the importance of their employees to the store's success, spotlighting their valued service in numerous news releases and articles over the years. Demonstrations of concern also included cards, visits, and flowers when employees and their families had an occasion of celebration or mourning; remembrance of employees' birthdays over the store's loudspeaker and a day's holiday from work; and financial aid for those with money problems.[51]

Personnel policies for employees, although reflecting Carlos' influence, became more complex during Alex's tenure. With the opening of the new store in 1951, a Mr. Picksley assumed the combined role of manager of employee relations and floor walker. Under his direction, recruitment for jobs at the store continued to be informal, with most prospective employees learning about jobs from a friend or relative. An emphasis on the store's history characterized the orientation of new employees. Most training was done on the job, but Enriqueta Martinez DeMeester remembers a tuition refund on schooling before the advent of Mr. Picksley. Discipline and employee complaints were handled first by Picksley and then by Alex. There were no written performance evaluations, but if an employee was to be fired, Alex had the last say. One cause

for dismissal was an infraction of the dress code or neglect of personal hygiene. One employee remembers Alex
calling her into his office and telling her to get a
deodorant in cosmetics and to take it to a certain salesgirl. The employee was to recommend to the salesgirl that
she take the deodorant to the restroom and apply it or go
home. Rules for drug and alcohol usage increased in severity as the store moved through the decade of the 1960s.[52]

Employee benefits included the standard holidays,
health insurance, discounts of cost plus 10 percent for
employees and cost plus 25 percent for an employee's
family, and bonuses at the end of the year to those department heads showing a profit. Raises were informally administered throughout the year. Management either called
employees in to inform them of a raise or just put it in
their paycheck. Jacome's began a profit-sharing program in
1951-1952, with a five-year eligibility stipulation for all
employees. By September, 1957, the fund stood at
$86,145.[53] Alex called it "just a little nest egg for you
guys in case something happens."[54] This made employees
much more aware of waste and its effect on store profits.
Credit Manager DeMeester remembers saving paper clips,
something she was not prone to do before the program
began.[55]

Store policies governing merchandising and customer
relations changed under Alex's management but were still

highly personalized, with concern for the individual customer a primary goal. The store continued to adhere to Carlos' edict against handling inferior merchandise. Bargain basements specializing in seconds or irregular merchandise were making their way into department stores across the nation as a way to decrease expenses,[56] but Jacome's never considered this a viable option.[57] If customers did return merchandise considered inferior, the clerks were instructed to take the article back in a pleasant manner. As Alex explained to consumer advocate Ralph Nader in a 1976 letter thanking him for "making manufacturers or wholesalers offer first quality merchandise only and marking inferior merchandise plainly as inferior or seconds . . . in eighty years we have made good on any type of merchandise returned to us by customers."[58]

"The customer is always right," governed relationships between customers and clerks.[59] Individual departments offered different services. The lingerie department, for example, was most eager to special order individual garments for any customer. Specialized ordering was predicated on the assumption that if the customers came into the store to make such an order, they would visit other departments as well. The return visit to pick up the order was a second chance for customers to buy other items. Psychologically, as well, management considered the good will this special service generated and the additional purchases that would undoubtedly result.[60] The hosiery department offered another special service, a discount for customers after the purchase of three pairs of hose.[61]

Other store policies governing customer relations covered the stock room, sales and their promotion, and special services. In the stock room, "large orders for ranchers in Mexico, humble orders for the religious in Arizona, and ordinary orders for charge customers received equal and special attention." Scheduled by the buyer, sales were "authentic" in that merchandise was not purchased for the event and then marked down. They usually occurred after a seasonal inventory and a quarterly sales report.[62] Catalogues advertising these sales were mailed to regular customers far in advance of the broad public promotion.[63] Jacome's instituted a special service for customers living in the Fort Huachuca, Arizona, area. Without cost to customers, they could use a special telephone line and place orders with the store's personal shopper.[64] Tucson patrons needing postal service could utilize the United States post office substation located on the lower level of the store.[65]

These policies and others developed a devoted clientele. Years later, customers explained how they could never leave the store empty-handed. A case in point was columnist and former governor of Arizona, Howard Pyle. During his first gubernatorial campaign, after a long day of walking, he entered the store. With Alex at his side, Pyle proceeded through the store, shaking hands, ending up at the men's shoe department. Before he knew it, Alex was measuring him for a pair of shoes and telling him "that was the least he could do for his campaign . . . give him something easy to walk in."[66]

Unique advertising such as the 1951 non-commercial Christmas also had customer appeal. As described in *Women's Wear Daily*, Jacome's refrained from any active advertising on the week preceding Christmas and used for their display a religious motif instead of the traditional Santa Claus.[67] Under the heading, "One Tucson Businessman Puts Christ Back into Christmas," the *Arizona Daily Star* described the painting used for the display: a Renaissance masterpiece by Il Bassano (originally thought to be by Tintoretto), the "Adoration of the Shepherds," loaned to Jacome's by the Knoedler Galleries of New York.[68] As a result of nationwide coverage, Jacome's received letters on their innovative Christmas display from across the United States.[69]

With planned obsolescence of fashion exploiting the status market for a greater turnover of goods, customers had grown to expect a wide variety of styles. This brought an enormous increase in the number of items in stock, from a few hundred in 1896 to about 140,000 in 1957.[70] For example, Jacome's carried four nationally advertised brands

of hosiery and five brands of brassieres. A single manufacturer, Maidenform, offered one hundred different styles
of brassieres from which buyers could choose.[71] Thus
buyers found advanced planning a necessity for the next
season.[72] Because Tucson was still remote from the style
centers, townspeople acknowledged that they wore out-of-
date fashion longer than persons living in cities such as
San Francisco, New York, or even Houston. But Jacome's
women customers had a growing awareness of the new styles,
and the store's buyers increasingly worked to stay abreast
of the trends.[73]

If managing to stay on top of the growing number of
styles was not enough, the buyer also had to take into
account several other factors: customers' wants and requests, the history of past sales for each class of merchandise, what was currently selling, the stock sold by
competitors, items leading in current sales volume and
future projections, and probable local purchasing power in
relation to commodity prices.[74] To accommodate all these
conditions, the buyers kept extensive records, met with
salespersons from the different houses in both spring and
fall when they visited the store, and made buying trips to
Los Angeles and New York. They also pored over pamphlets,
catalogues, price lists, pictures, samples, and other
informational material sent them by the wholesalers.[75]

By systematically balancing the relationship between stock and sales in order to achieve the largest profit, Jacome's maintained control of this vast inventory.[76] To that end they developed an accounting system which quickly adapted to constant changes and which enabled them "to determine the cost value of the closing inventory without actually counting stocks."[77] Unlike Carlos, Alex and his managerial staff did not need to take a complete physical inventory at the end of the year. According to Mildred Devine, A University of Arizona student researching Jacome's inventory control system in 1959, "With each department charged with a certain amount of merchandise and with a book inventory of these different units readily available," Jacome management could "interpret methods of operations monthly, quarterly, and semiannually." And under this system, "sick" departments with poor control of their merchandise were readily diagnosed.[78]

Increasing stock meant a need for more space. With less than five years in their new building, Jacome's acquired 12,000 additional square feet by expanding in 1957. Both the first and second floors were extended forty feet to the north while J. C. Penney's installed a new store next door. The Steinfeld family financed, built, and leased both structures for twenty-five years with a twenty-year option. The new selling space replaced Steinfeld's original buildings, a wholesale hardware store constructed in 1917, and the Pioneer Garage and Standard Oil service station built in 1929. Further concentration of the retail portion of downtown Tucson in the Stone and Pennington area was at the core of the plan. According to Harold Steinfeld, "the more competitive stores we can center around this retail hub, the more advantageous it will be for the shopping public. . . . Our own store and our competitors will both prosper by this move, and customers will be better served."[79]

With the expansion of 1957, Jacome's instituted a cost saving device reminiscent of the store's early days: putting the stock on full display. Self-service features were introduced in the budget lingerie and dress sections, but other departments in the store were rearranged so that sales persons had surplus stock close by and could easily replenish the display stocks.[80] Movable fixtures gave additional flexibility to merchandise display.

Before the opening of their newly expanded store, Jacome's ran a series of articles in the *Arizona Daily Star* on the history of the store.[81] Responding to a customer's letter on the series, Alex stated that when he "first planned the series it was with the intention of acquainting our customers with the fact that the policies of our founder have not been changed one iota with all our expansion."[82] In response to a similar letter from newspaper commentator and rabid anti-New Dealer, Westbrook Pegler,

Alex outlined another motivation for running the series. He stated, "There is the need to keep our family together as a new generation comes along. I thought a history of this sort would tend to bring us closer together."[83] In this letter to Pegler, Alex also expressed negative thoughts about the expansion. He emphasized that "the terrific taxes we are paying today at all levels . . . have killed just about all the incentive and initiative you need to enlarge a business." Prophetically, he also explained, "We just had to expand in order to keep pace with competition." Apparently, Alex and Pegler, who settled in Tucson in the early 1940s, enjoyed an on-going relationship based on their mutual appraisal of the national economic scene as well as an antipathy toward communists.[84] Nowhere in their correspondence, however, is found the vehemence toward Eleanor Roosevelt and the United Nations which Pegler regularly expressed in his columns.

Alex's explanation to Pegler on the necessity of expansion to meet competition is more fully explained in an article published in 1958 by the *Arizona Business and Economic Review* entitled, "Downtown Tucson and the Woman Shopper." Finding shopping downtown a pleasant experience for most shoppers, the author of the article, Daniel W. Raaf, cited several adverse factors beginning to affect shopping there. Among other things, he mentioned traffic and parking conditions, distance of residences from the downtown area, and the tendency of newer residents to shop downtown less. According to Raaf, this last trend "may have more significance in the long run for both the downtown area and future outlying shopping centers."[85] Raaf had a good point. Newer residents in Pima County were beginning to outnumber the old, with the population standing at 141,216 in 1950 and growing to 265,660 by 1960.[86] Even more to the point, many of the customers of stores in the outlying shopping centers were already coming from those residential areas around them.[87]

Traffic problems were also increasing downtown, with ingress and egress still a growing problem. In order to cope with that situation, the City tried many approaches. In 1953, for example, a one-way street plan went into effect downtown.[88] Traffic snarls occurred on the first day.[89] In order to prevent traffic jams, the City restricted parking on Stone Avenue.[90] In 1957, plans were developed to open and widen the streets as well as to make more use of the Freeway to the south of the main business district.[91]

If difficulties in driving into and out of downtown existed, the parking conditions were even worse. In 1954, the National Safety Council cited Tucson for the safety of its streets and warned that more parking space was needed downtown.[92] In order to alleviate the parking problem, Tucson's downtown retailers inaugurated in 1956 a "Ride and

Shop" program designed to induce customers to utilize the city buses and leave their automobiles at home. This supplemented the "Park and Shop" program to encourage downtown shopping, which was already in effect.[93] During that same time period, Leon Levy made a futile proposal to downtown landlords, the Ivancovich family, for construction of a parking garage.[94] Retailers knew that improved bus service was one way to solve part of the problem, and the Tucson Rapid Transit did its part to help. It changed its bus service to the periphery of downtown in 1959 to bring customers closer to their destination. It also expanded its schedules on the evenings downtown stores stayed open for the added convenience of customers.[95] Yet, the problems continued to grow.

Increased traffic and parking problems in the 1950s did not immediately put a damper on the renovation and construction taking place in the downtown area. A new Lerner's store appeared at Stone and Congress. Further north on Stone the Tucson Newspapers, Inc., constructed a new plant. Across the street from Jacome's, Steinfeld's placed on their roof a hugh sixty-foot electric sign of a pioneer driving his wagon and oxen. In 1955, they completely remodeled their store.[96] Continuing their expansion of the 1930s and 1940s, Levy's opened a beautiful new store at Pennington and Scott in 1950 and added a third floor three years later.[97] When Aaron Levy died in 1958, his brother, Leon, assumed the presidency of the store and continued to cast about for other expansion opportunities. When fire swept through Cele Peterson's store in 1956, she squelched rumors that she planned to move to the growing east side of town by resuming business on East Pennington.[98] The same year as the fire, Dave Bloom, in the midst of remodeling his store for an expansion of the lower level, died, leaving the store to his three sons, Dave, Herb, and Ted.[99]

Short-term optimism of independent retailers in downtown Tucson did nothing to halt the growth of factors beginning to operate against them. Besides ingress and egress and parking problems, downtown properties were beginning to deteriorate.[100] Most importantly, nationwide conditions spelled trouble. Every city in the United States witnessed the proliferation of shopping centers and the restructuring of retailing through the growth of conventional and discount chains. Retailers in Tucson's central business district, "seeing first of all the conditions of [their] own industry in the local market,"[101] only came to realize the full significance of this concentration process when one of their own broke ranks to join the chain store movement.

CHAPTER SIX

THE GRANDE DAME STRIPPED OF HER JEWELS

In 1960, an article in the *Arizona Review* raised the question confronting Jacome's and other independent retailers across the United States in the coming decades: Did concentration in the industry spell the end of many of them? Citing the bitter Depression-era struggle for survival between chain stores and independent retailers, the article pointed to many signs that indicated the battle was escalating. The chains, especially discounters, continued to wage war against fair trade laws and other legislation passed to protect small retailers. Congressional attention focused upon collusion between lending agencies and major retailers because of charges that dominant firms had reserved prime shopping center locations and made them inaccessible to smaller stores. Independents were also finding it increasingly difficult to compete with the chain stores' mass media advertising and the price advantages they enjoyed from the manufacturers.[1]

When Levy's joined the holding company known as Federated Department Stores in 1960 and at the same time planned to open its first store outside the central business district, the first real wave of concern spread through downtown Tucson. Up to that point, retailers in the downtown area, exerting power and influence far beyond their numbers, had exhibited more concern with conditions in the local community than with those nationwide. The Penney's and Sears chains had located downtown years earlier, and retailers had come to accept their existence as part of Tucson life. Shopping centers on the outskirts of town offered some competition, but downtown retailers remained complacent in the knowledge that they were the center of retailing activity. Much of their complacency came from knowledge that industrial growth did not accompany Tucson's tremendous expansion after World War II, and thus they remained geographically and economically isolated from the mainstream of American economic life and the vast changes taking place there.

Levy's move, however, symbolized the onset of a new era in the "Old Pueblo," whether the retailers wanted it or not. C. Wright Mills provided an accurate portrait of Tucson's power structure before and after the pending change in his 1956 portrayal of American power elite. According to Mills, traditionally a "set of cliques or crowds" composed of old upper-class people in the community had sat at the top of local society, judging and deciding the important community issues. These cliques, which in the case of Tucson were heavily dominated by downtown retailers, identified their principal socio-economic interests with the immediate area. With the arrival of national corporations and their executives with interests regional and national in scope, local cliques were displaced. From that point on it became evident that to "remain merely local was to fail" as these corporate executives with national status assumed central positions of power and authority in the community.[2]

Leon Levy's awareness of this nationwide shifting of power from local influentials to the corporate managerial elite and the parallels he might have drawn in relation to Tucson is open to question. Certainly the reasons he gave for joining Federated reflected a personal realization that in economic terms local independent department stores were losing power. As he stated, "Taxes were eating the store up and we could not borrow the funds to continue to expand and grow."[3] In a business where strategic location is necessary for survival, Levy saw the downtown area beginning to lose its vitality and felt expansion beyond its borders was essential. Besides the favored status chains enjoyed in capital markets, Levy probably had another reason for joining Federated: scale economies afforded it by the national parent company in everything from distribution systems, buying practices, and management training to advertising programs and computer technology.[4]

To the downtown retailers, Levy's expansion plans were "old news." As early as 1958, the store had announced plans to branch out, initially choosing a site at Broadway and Wilmot. When these plans fell through shortly after Aaron Levy's death, Leon closed a deal with the owners of the El Con Shopping Center for a store to open in 1960. At the same time, Levy's went public, selling stock first to employees at $17 to $18 per share.

What surprised the downtown merchant community was Levy's announcement that they planned to join Federated. According to Leon Levy, the initial contact from the chain came shortly after he returned from Europe in January of 1960. Meeting with Fred Lazarus and John Lavor of Federated, Levy received an interesting offer, which he explored further with Lavor over a three-day period. After this initial session, certain questions about the venture continued to concern him. For instance, would Levy employees receive full credit for their years of service when absorbed into the Federated pension plan? With the resolution of this and other problems in the ensuing months, Levy's and Federated signed the papers closing the deal on August 1, 1960, at the Pioneer Hotel. Two months later the El Con store opened.[5]

As the 1960s advanced and other major businesses followed Levy's lead into the east and north sections of the city, Alex looked to business organizations and political entities to stem the "pressure from outlying competition," which was affecting his trade. To Lee Davis, chairman of the Tucson Trade Bureau Promotional Committee, he protested the discontinuance of "Downtown Wednesday Only Specials" which had drawn customers to the area.[6] He also requested free parking for customers from Tucson's Mayor and Council "because the majority of businesses require foot traffic to survive, whether a Central Business District or a Shopping Center."[7] Letters to state legislators directly attacked the chain stores, with Alex suggesting "Sunday closing laws . . . [because the] . . . big chain stores were promoting Sunday more than ever."[8]

Alex's appeal for help from local and state government did not signify that he viewed them as benefactors. On the contrary, while looking to the government for political help, Alex took a view of the state that was an interesting blend of "the Latin tradition" and opinions long held by small businessmen. In both cases, the state was seen as having only negative functions: to regulate and to tax.[9]

Like the businessmen of his father's generation, Alex also expressed strong beliefs in the free enterprise system and the operation of supply and demand in a competitive market. It is not clear how he reconciled his belief in competitive free enterprise and his support of fair trade laws legalizing price-fixing to avoid "ruinous competition."[10] Nor did he explain how he viewed the chains', under the guise of competition, erosion of his participation in the free market system. Perhaps like other American businessmen, Alex wanted not so much a "free" enterprise system but a "safe" free market for his particular business.

Yet he insisted that promotion of a competitive free enterprise system, both at home and abroad, was central to his political philosophy. When discussing United States expansion in international trade, for example, he urged the "promotion of the private enterprise system . . . to counter the Red."[11] The same fear of Communist influence marked his views on domestic labor movements. Of particular interest was his belief that Cesar Chavez, labor organizer of farm workers in the San Joaquin Valley of California, was a Communist. Chavez's movement represented a real threat to the established social system of which the Jacome family had become a part. In a real sense, Chavez's questioning of the rationales by which local ethnic stratifications were maintained presented a challenge not only to American agribusiness but also to those like the Jacome family who had risen within the system.[12]

His views on bilingual programs closely corresponded to his general political philosophy. Although more conservative than views on bilingualism generally expressed by the Hispanic business community, they contained some of the same concerns. Most leading Hispanics felt that Hispanic students needed a strong English language competency to compete in the business world. At the same time they urged that strengthening bilingual skills would prove advantageous in the international marketplace. Citing his own experience, Alex maintained that bilingual programs were not in the best interests of the Hispanic child. Spanish was spoken in his home, but at school he had no problem learning "English and other courses offered."[13] A 1.3 million dollar grant awarded by the Ford Foundation to the La Raza Council for bilingual programs drew his special attention because he feared the program would "segregate and harm the Mexicans more than ever."[14] Similarly, in a letter to Senator Paul Fannin, he opposed the 1975 Voting Rights Act providing that ballots and election material must be bilingual.[15]

Civil Rights activities and the movement for bilingualism also popularized new descriptive terms for Mexican-Americans. Alex's reaction to those terms gives a strong indication of his identification with his culture. On October 29, 1976, The University of Arizona's College of Liberal Arts Committee on Mexican American Studies published a "Noticiero Chicano," with articles containing such terms as "Chicano" and "La Raza." Upon receipt of the publication, Alex drafted a letter to Paul Rosenblatt, Dean of the College, stating, "If Arizona State can use the words, 'Spanish Surnamed' . . . I think the University of Arizona should eliminate the use of the word 'Chicano' or

'Raza.'"[16]   Reflecting the sentiments of an earlier era when President Theodore Roosevelt coined the phrase "hyphenated Americans," Alex clarified his cultural identification in a letter to Senator Fannin. "Don't misunderstand me," he stated, "I am proud of my Mexican ancestry, but first of all I am an American and there is no hyphenation to it, just like the Italians, Danes, English and others who changed their names and became American."[17]

The Civil Rights activism of the 1960s produced legislation which increased governmental regulation of the store's personnel practices. Title VII of the Civil Rights Act of 1964 and Executive Orders decreeing Affirmative Action programs, according to Alex F. Jacome, Jr., took "lots of extra time . . . especially in terms of paperwork." The dress styles and grooming of those entering the work force during the turbulent sixties also led to a stiffening of policies governing the store's dress code. No longer could men wear beards or hair below their collars, and women were required to wear clothing deemed appropriate to their sex. Yet, for women, this dress code broadened from the 1950s edict of only black or navy blue dresses to a variety of colors and even pants.[18]

Jacome's continued to look for sales personnel to fit the profile developed by its founder many decades earlier, with loyalty and honesty high on the list of desired attributes. In so doing, the store was going against the nationwide trend, especially among the chains, of recruiting a low-skilled, high-turnover work force in order to reduce costs.[19] Carlos could have written Alex's answer to a student in merchandising about the personal characteristics and attitudes Jacome's looked for when hiring workers: "show imagination . . . hard work . . . and be honest and above reproach."[20] Training for employees emphasized what Carlos had instilled in his children many years ago: "Make your store a friendly store and it will live forever."[21] Yet customer complaints indicated that some personnel no longer adhered to that principle. "Jacome's isn't the friendly store it used to be" wrote one customer in 1967.[22] To a similar complaint about an employee, Alex replied, "I'm sorry one of the many Jacomes was not around to be of help."[23]

Theft and wage problems also surfaced in employee relations. The pension fund, based as it was on profits, made employees acutely aware of thefts. With the move to Pennington and Stone, however, the store had to employ undercover agents to monitor the sales help from time to time. Customer theft was also a problem. At Christmas time, off-duty police were utilized to prevent shoplifting. Curtains were shortened in the women's dressing rooms for better visibility, and the number of clothes a person could take into a fitting room was restricted.[24]

Blaming the inflation and recession of the early 1970s on Richard Nixon wanting "to be reelected," Alex wrote Arizona Senator Barry Goldwater that "Jacome's employees want a wage hike, the auto workers got theirs and the steel workers got theirs. Where is this going to stop?" Although Goldwater's reply to this particular letter is not known, these two heirs of Arizona department store magnates corresponded regularly through the years sharing similar views on a diversity of subjects. Whether discussing politics, foreign policy, or a multitude of other questions, they displayed an obvious intimacy in their correspondence which reflected a long-standing relationship. For instance, in 1962, Goldwater was aiming for the Republican presidential nomination which apparently would place him in the running against the Democratic incumbent, President John F. Kennedy. After a Saturday night speech, Alex sent him a letter saying, "I hope you won't mind a little fatherly advice . . . in criticizing the Democrats I am afraid you lose friends," because they like Catholics and Jews hate to be damned. In the same letter he also suggested that Goldwater "not mention Mrs. Kennedy, unless she commits a major crime. Your remarks regarding her were a little too vituperous (sic)." In 1963, before the Kennedy assassination, Goldwater complained to Alex about President Kennedy's Latin American policy, saying that the administration's total emphasis on economic aid would not solve the problem.[25]

In contrast to their similar political views, the Senator and Alex took divergent paths in matters of business management. Goldwater's Department Store abandoned its family-owned and family-operated origins in the early 1960s and joined a chain, the Associated Dry Goods Corporation. Operating a number of select department stores from New York to Los Angeles, Associated was one of a number of groups which exercised financial control over its stores while allowing each to retain its individual character and personality.[26]

Although chain stores like Goldwater's and Levy's were moving away from the family-oriented attitudes of small business from which they sprang, family continued to dominate Jacome's management. Seeking to rationalize their management structure, chains were wooing graduates from prestigious business schools to their management teams.[27] For example, shortly after joining Federated, Leon Levy brought Henry Quinto into Levy's management. Quinto, a highly experienced Harvard graduate and former employee of the Allied Stores Corporation, became Executive Vice President for the store and assumed the presidency in 1967. Together with Leon Levy, he helped to elaborate explicit goals and procedures which replaced what had been, for the most part, unwritten policies. Levy's also increased executive salaries to attract others with credentials like those of Quinto.[28]

While management of Jacome's remained under family control, both the family and the store managers were changing. In 1962, the popular merchandising manager and Alex's right-hand man, Richard Jacome, died. He was the twelfth of Carlos' and Dionisia's children.[29] Three years later, the oldest, Carlos, Jr., died in Seattle, Washington, where he had moved at an early age.[30] By 1972, six of Alex's brothers and sisters were gone, and another generation of Jacomes was taking over the store's operation. Moving up in the ranks was Alex's son, Alex F. Jacome, Jr., promoted to sales manager and assistant to the merchandising manager in 1967. At the same time, Richard C. Jacome, Jr., became divisional merchandise manager of domestics and housewares, and Henry G. Jacome, Jr., assumed management of the men's furnishings and clothing departments.[31] In 1972, Alex, Sr., stepped down as president of Jacome's and became Chairman of the Board. His son, Alex, Jr., succeeded him.[32]

Throughout the 1960s, management of the store brought excellent profits, which peaked at an all-time high of $4,000,000 in 1967. While on a buying trip to Europe in April, 1968, Alex, Sr., received a letter from the store's comptroller, Gilbert Martinez, describing the "unusually busy April . . . [with a] 28% increase in sales."

According to Martinez, income taxes and the pension fund took a total of $132,000, but the import shop alone grossed $9,000.[33]

One reason for the store's continued prosperity was its mastery of marketing techniques. Jacome's utilized Spanish and English language newspapers in Mexico to promote its merchandise.[34] It capitalized on what other stores might have considered unfortunate experiences. For example, the *Department Store Journal* demonstrated how the store's advertising made almost everyone in Tucson aware that the popular piece goods and notions departments had been moved from a central location to an out-of-the-way space in the basement.[35] The store sent customers special materials reminding them of its long tradition. Of special importance here was a "First Day of Issue" envelope with a Commemorative Stamp bearing Carlos' portrait as a member of the Constitutional Convention in 1912 to celebrate the fiftieth anniversary of Arizona statehood.[36] Jacome's also conveyed a strong emotional message of attachment to its customers when in 1975 it began a special shopping day before Christmas for the physically handicapped. Established in honor of Alex, Jr.'s son, Gilberto A. Jacome, this day gave the physically handicapped in Tucson an opportunity "to do their Christmas shopping without having to contend with the hustle and bustle of the holiday crowds."[37]

The same year Jacome's profits peaked, Levy's announced a new five million dollar department store at the El Con shopping center and mentioned Jacome's as a possible tenant for its existing store. The *Tucson Daily Citizen* reported on September 27, 1967, that "President Alex G. Jacome said today he has talked with El Con developers of the shopping center about taking over the Levy store, 'but only in general terms.' Jacome's has another thirteen years on a lease for its Stone Avenue store, which Jacome said continues to be a profitable business."[38]

Several factors supported a move to El Con. This was not the first time Jacome's had thought of opening another branch. As early as 1928, Carlos indicated "he was contemplating opening other stores." During that period of time, Carlos and Alex went to Phoenix to look at a specific site, were wined and dined by the property owners, and then decided after retiring to their hotel for the night that they had enough problems in Tucson. The next day the stock market crashed.[39]

Also, the proposed move to El Con was one customers and competitors supported.[40] Henry Quinto personally took Alex through the old Levy's store and suggested he could "stay downtown and die on the vine, or come to El Con and take his chances." According to Quinto, Levy's motive for inviting in a competitor was the need for a strong anchor on the other side of the mall.[41] Herb Bloom, who together with his brothers had opened a second store at El Con in 1963, also talked to both Alex and his son about taking the old Levy location. According to Bloom, he really "put the heat on because he wanted a local store close to their shop."[42]

Yet Jacome's resisted. As Alex explained to a customer, we would have to "borrow most of the capital to launch the enterprise" and splitting the business between the two stores would probably yield no profit.[43] The Steinfeld lease on the downtown store, which stipulated that Jacome's could not have another store within fifteen miles, was another major problem. Years later, Steinfeld's Jim Davis acknowledged that if Jacome's had challenged the lease in court, they might have broken it. There were precedents in other states. On the other hand, he believed Steinfeld's could have persuaded Jacome's not to go to El Con since it was only three miles away.[44]

Jacome's was offered the Levy building on a lease at $1.25 a square foot.[45] According to Holden Olsen, Executive Loan Officer with the Southern Arizona Bank, Alex did discuss the offer with people in the bank office. In Holden's opinion, he could have acquired necessary interim bank financing if he had secured permanent financing from an insurance company. Except for occasional extensions of pay-off dates on outstanding notes, Jacome's credit record with the bank was fairly good. Olsen also felt Alex probably would have won approval of the interim bank loan at one-half percent over par, something Alex demanded and usually got because of his personal relationship with the bank president. Yet, to Olsen's knowledge, the El Con offer never reached the loan proposal stage.[46] Alex hired an appraiser from California to look at the old Levy store. Taking this man's advice, he called the El Con Center owner and said, "We pass."[47]

In February, 1968, Levy's closed the downtown store and on September 16, 1969, opened a six-million dollar, 225,000 square foot structure at the new location in El Con.[48] Built on the site of the old El Con Hotel,[49] the store opening was celebrated with several parties. There was a press preview luncheon attended by representatives from several nationally known publications and a champagne party featuring a well-known Hollywood personality, Cary Grant.[50] A few months later, Levy's announced they were considering two more suburban stores, one ten miles east of the El Con site and the other ten miles west.[51] Construction of a west-side store followed in 1982, but the east-side location remained undeveloped as late as 1985.

The disintegration of the central business district, almost coinciding with the El Con Shopping Center opening in 1960, continued relentlessly after Levy's closing of its downtown store. Survival of the remaining businesses required a number of strategic changes. Most pressing was the need for cohesive action to deal with problems such as parking, advertising, zoning, and taxes. Yet, as reported by the *Daily News Record* in 1972, downtown retailers had made little progress.[52] A 1979 headline in the *Arizona Daily Star* declaring, "Retailers admit infighting slows downtown plans," showed little had changed in almost two decades.[53]

Number one on the agenda of problems was parking. Downtown customers had to search for a parking space and if lucky enough to find one, then deal with a parking meter. They encountered neither problem at a shopping center. Further, the Tucson Police Department was notorious for its tight control of downtown parking. Cele Peterson remembers, with chagrin, arriving at her place of business only to find an illegally parked vehicle blocking her private alleyway. When she resorted to parking in front of her store, she found that like her customers, she was frequently ticketed by the diligent Tucson Police.[54]

Other problems faced by downtown merchants were taxes, deteriorating buildings, zoning ordinances, and loss of the Mexican trade. According to Cele Peterson, one of the reasons for property deterioration, especially on Congress Street, was the high taxation the City of Tucson levied on any improvements to buildings. A strict enforcement of zoning ordinances presented store owners difficulties as well. For instance, a requirement of two fire exits per store made surveillance for theft very difficult. Similar regulations at El Con were much less rigorously enforced.[55]

Probably the biggest blow to Jacome's was the drying up of the Mexican trade. Some of the contributors to that decline were the Pioneer International Hotel fire, the requirement that Mexican customers pay sales taxes, withdrawal of free parking stamps to Mexican customers, and the drop of the Mexican peso. The Pioneer fire occurred on December 20, 1970, and destroyed the major residence for Mexican tourists coming to Tucson.[56] Shortly afterwards, Mexican tourists encountered a sales tax from which they had previously been exempt. To make matters worse, Tucson's Mayor and Council withdrew the free parking stamps Mexican customers had grown to expect. One of the strongest proponents of these changes was a Hispanic Councilman, Reuben Romero, who contended the well-to-do Mexicans who shopped in Tucson could afford to pay.[57] Finally came the devaluation of the Mexican peso in August of 1976. When the peso, which had been pegged to the United States dollar for twenty-two years, was allowed to float, purchases of everything "from clothing to tractors by Mexicans who frequented Tucson retailers dropped 25 percent and more."[58]

In addition to those problems, downtown business owners suffered from the repeal of federal and state fair trade laws. These laws had prohibited discounters from undercutting the manufacturer's retail price. In December, 1975, President Gerald Ford signed the Consumer Goods Pricing Act of 1975 which terminated all interstate utilization of "fair trade" or resale price maintenance. During the 1975 Arizona legislative session, both the House and the Senate passed repeal measures, but the Conference Committee could not resolve differences between the two measures. With passage of the federal law, however, the Arizona fair trade legislation also ended. In their long campaign for change, the discounters argued that the laws conflicted with a free market, sustained inflation, and in the last analysis were unconstitutional. Until repeal, discounters had carried products with unfamiliar labels and unknown quality. After repeal, they expanded their product lines and broadened their target customer population, drawing from the former middle-class customers of conventional retail stores like Jacome's.[59]

Recognizing the value of fair trade laws, Jacome's had supported their enforcement in the Tucson area. When Korby's, the first mini-department store to locate outside the downtown area in 1951, was said to be selling national brands such as Van Heusen and Haggar at lower prices, Jacome's and other retailers complained to the manufacturers, threatening to withdraw their business. The owners of Korby's, Nathan and Flo Kaiserman, resolved that controversy by showing copies of their newspaper advertisements to the manufacturers. Their ads proved they were not selling below the suggested retail price. Still, in the years that followed, local retailers kept a close vigilance over the actions of their competitors to ensure that these laws were observed.[60]

Fair trade repeal was only one of a long list of reasons downtown retailers had for looking at the question of their very survival. Most of them concluded that their only course was to move out of downtown. In 1963, Dave Bloom and Sons expanded to El Con and in 1965 closed the downtown store.[61] Steinfeld's, rather than Jacome's opened their El Con store in the old Levy building in March of 1971.[62] Like the Bloom brothers, Cele Peterson saw her customers moving to the east side of town and heard from them the difficulties of getting downtown. She opened an El Con store the same year as the Blooms, and in the first year her business went up over 30 percent. Unlike the Blooms, she maintained her downtown store until one more parking ticket provoked her to close in 1979. By the time she left, the only remaining retail stores of consequence were Jacome's, Penney's, and Lerner's.[63]

In 1976, Jacome's apparently found a way to bypass the fifteen-mile stipulation in the Steinfeld lease by going outside Tucson to Sierra Vista, Arizona, for their second location. Optimistically announcing that "there undoubtedly will be more to come," store management signed the lease for a 65,000 square foot structure and hired architect Terry Atkinson to draw up plans for the internal allocation of space.[64] Problems with the Sierra Vista city government led to the postponement of the opening planned in August. Cancelling merchandise offers, they rescheduled for March, 1977. Again unable to open, Jacome's dropped the Sierra Vista project altogether. The developer sued for breach of contract, but after a court trial Jacome's emerged the winner.[65]

Still searching for a site, they discussed terms with the owner of Park Mall, the second major shopping center to appear in Tucson. Small space allocation, 30,000 square feet as compared with Sears' 225,000 square feet, led them to look elsewhere. In turn, they gave close scrutiny to Phoenix, El Paso, and Green Valley.[66]

At the same time Jacome management spent many hours talking with bankers about expansion. What they encountered in trying to obtain capital for expansion characterized the plight of independent retailers across the United States. Typically, family-run independents were generating inadequate retained earnings to expand. In fact, as inflation soared and recession grew in 1974 and 1975, all but the very healthiest had to cut their operations drastically. Like other independents, Jacome's found the bank willing to lend for operating capital but not for expansion. In advising them to focus on what they already had, the bank officials also suggested a reduction of expenses by shutting down one floor of the store. Because the overhead would remain the same, according to Alex F. Jacome, Jr., this afforded no savings for the store.[67]

Jacome's had at least one other alternative to expansion. According to Alex F. Jacome, Jr., "Over the years the store had several inquiries from the chains." However, Alex, Sr., felt that acquisition of the firm by a department store chain represented a "betrayal of the family name and the integrity and honesty it represented."[68]

In all probability, this decision to ignore the chains' overtures reflected the influence of culture on Jacome's survival. Certainly the admonitions of Carlos to his children about integrity and honesty in business played a strong role in the decision not to consider joining a chain. Just as important was the precedence family interests took over the maximum exploitation of economic opportunities. Some experts have argued that the exceptionally strong "familistic" trait within the Mexican-American culture curtails mobility by sustaining emotional attachments to people, places, and things. As a source of collective pride, "familism" is ultimately the cause of resistance to change of all sorts.[69] At Jacome's, protection of the family and its name rested upon a management structure in which the family members assumed the positions of trust.

Rationalized chain management would have eroded that control. Increased risk to the family name and managerial
depersonalization were avenues they chose not to pursue.

By late 1979, Jacome's had almost reached final
agreement for the opening of two stores outside the downtown area. One, a grocery building in the Casas Adobes
Shopping Center, had 16,000 square feet and offered space
for a scaled-down version of the Pennington and Stone
store. A second site in Green Valley, like the Casas Adobe
store, required a minimum amount of capital investment to
open. Inflation aborted those plans and forced Jacome's to
make preparations for liquidation in early 1980.[70]

On January 15, 1980, Alex, Sr., arrived at the
store as usual, greeted employee Armando Flores with his
"usual smile and a good morning," and went to his office.[71]
While working at his desk, he complained of chest pains and
collapsed. His son attempted to revive him until para-
medics arrived to take him to St. Mary's Hospital. There
Alex was pronounced dead upon arrival of a massive heart
attack.[72]

"He died the way he wanted to, working in the
office, with his boots on," said his daughter, Margarita.
"He was the patriarch," stated Alex, Jr.; "he not only ran
the business, but the family as well--and that is kind of
difficult for a number ten."[73] Remaining were two sisters,
Josephine and Rose, and four brothers, Henry, Arthur,

Augustine, and John.[74] Friends and relatives from throughout Arizona, the United States, and Mexico came to Tucson
for the funeral mass held at St. Augustine Cathedral.[75]

During the last years of his life, Alex had continued to receive honors from the community. In 1974 The
University of Arizona awarded him an honorary Doctor of Law
degree for his "achievements in business and civic affairs
and in the field of international relations." In 1976,
accompanied by his beautiful wife, Estela, he served as
Grand Marshal of the Fiesta de los Vaqueros Parade, an
event unique to the Tucson community. Commenting upon his
appointment as marshal, Arizona Governor Raul Castro noted,
"He typifies Tucson and has made our neighbors to the south
and southern Arizona become as one."[76]

In late February, six weeks after Alex's death, the
Jacome Department Store announced its closing because of
the declining retail market in downtown Tucson. The firm
was not going bankrupt, according to Alex, Jr., "it simply
wasn't making enough money." Stockholders, about a "dozen
family members," would receive the distribution of the
firm's assets. Although his father had made plans to
liquidate the store prior to his death, Alex, Jr.,
acknowledged, "I'm glad he is not around to see it . . .
after all, this was his whole life."[77]

On Thursday, March 6, 1980, the *Arizona Daily Star*
announced Jacome's "Out of Business" sale. The store

offered "every item from [a] $1.5 million inventory of fine fashions, Home Furnishings . . . Antiques and Collectibles . . . [at] 20% to 50% off." According to the advertisement, "lifetime savings were offered on America's most reputable famous brand labels," many of long standing at Jacome's: Society Brand, Arrow, Haggar, Farah, and, of course, Stetson.[78]

Employees at Jacome's, now numbering less than one hundred, felt a great sense of loss with the impending closing, and reactions were wide and varied.[79] Import shop manager, Grace Bourguignon, sensed it was coming even before the announcement because customers were treating her treasures differently. When the liquidators appeared, she refused to help them sell the articles she had pampered for so long.[80] Annie Shaar, an employee of thirty-eight years, noticed during the hectic activity of the first day of the sale that people in the store for the first time in years kept asking, "Annie, why are they doing this? Why is the store closing?" When she, in turn, asked why they no longer patronized the store, they typically replied that "they didn't come downtown because they did not want to fight the traffic."[81] Nina Avennenti, a twenty-one-year veteran of the store, recalled that when the auctioneer intervened to sell an alpaca blanket from Peru which was going for 40 percent of its retail value but which a customer wanted for less, she snatched it from the customer and "just walked away," only to sell it a few minutes later for the whole 40 percent.[82] Annie Shaar probably stated most succinctly what the others felt as the items for sale dwindled, "I feel like I'm losing my family, my home, and it's very hard for me."[83]

Jacome management worked to place each employee in another job. When Leon Levy called to offer his help, many went to his store.[84] Tony Anton recalled that Alex, Jr., and Henry, Sr., went around placing employees with other organizations and found two or three places for him. Because of his ample pension fund, however, Tony elected to take a few years off.[85] Other employees revealed that several had deep feelings about the pension fund, which helped them through various emergencies after the store closed.[86] And some found employer concern reaching beyond finding them a job and provision of a retirement benefit. For example, Augustine Jacome told Grace Bourguignon "to get a new knee cap" before the store insurance ran out. She left the store the same day, went to the hospital, and never returned.[87]

"Jacome's reaches the end with nothing but its dignity," read a *Tucson Daily Citizen* headline on the last day of the store's existence. Mirroring the community's emotional response to the store's demise, the *Citizen* described its last minutes of life. "It is 4:10 p.m. Friday, April 4, 1980. The department store at the corner of Stone Avenue and Pennington Street basks in the warmth of a bright springtime sun. It is a pleasant day to die." The *Citizen* article went on to describe the few articles left from the store's month-long close-out sale as "a cut above your standard sale merchandise." It also explained that "when you're competing not with the guy down the street, but with the suburban expansion that offers your customers the glossy malls and expensive parking lots that your location can't provide, being a cut above the rest just isn't enough."[88]

At 5:25 p.m. a woman's voice announced over the store's public address system: "Attention, Jacome's shoppers: The store will be closing in five minutes. Thank you for shopping at Jacome's." Henry Jacome, Jr., peeled a sale poster from the plate glass window, looked at it for a moment, and then commented, "Jacome's is no more." There were a few goodbyes to the store Carlos began so optimistically in 1896, and at "5:50 p.m. a key turned not only the tumblers of the lock to the store but the pages of the story of an era." Two of Carlos' grandsons, Henry and Alex, shook hands in final farewell tribute to "a grand (sic) dame stripped of her jewels and her kingdom, but not her dignity."[89] In the end, she had remained true to her founder's origins.

CHAPTER SEVEN

CONCLUSION

Within a few years of Jacome's closing the last
vestige of the old-time department stores, at one time
synonymous with retailing in Tucson, was gone. Meyerson's
Department Store, also located in downtown Tucson, had
closed in 1979. Steinfeld's found their move into Levy's
former quarters at El Con at best a qualified success.
Eventually closing the old store across from Jacome's at
Stone and Pennington, they developed three specialty stores
for women's wear in addition to the department store in El
Con. These were designed to replace the El Con store,
which was temporarily turned into a discount outlet until
its lease expired. In 1984, however, Steinfeld's announced
it would close all its stores after 130 years of business.[1]

About six months later, on May 17, 1985, the Tucson
press reported that Federated Department Stores planned to
change the name of Levy's to Sanger Harris when the remodeling of the El Con store was completed. Federated had
already stripped Levy's of its status as an independent
division in 1982 and put it under management of the Dallas-
based Sanger Harris division. Leon Levy's death on December 27, 1984, removed the last obstacle to the name change.
As chairman of Sanger Harris, Jack Miller acknowledged, "I

156

don't know if I would have had the courage to change the
name while he [Leon Levy] was living . . . but it was
impractical and costly to try to operate the stores in the
division under two names. . . . If we're not Levy's we
shouldn't try to be Levy's."[2]

Several other remarks by the Sanger Harris chairman
suggested that local interests no longer predominated in
the operation of the Tucson store. For instance, Levy's
staff was cut 32 percent, from 803 to 546 full-time jobs as
the buying, advertising, credit, and warehouse operations
were moved to Dallas. Some employees were offered trans-
fers, but according to Harris, "most did not want to leave
Tucson. . . . We made the cuts [in staff] as humanely as
possible."[3] These remarks reflect none of the personal
concern Jacome's and other local retailers like Leon Levy
had earlier demonstrated for displaced Jacome's Department
Store employees when the store closed. What they did
convey was the changing circumstances of Tucson's retailing
community in the 1980s.

The Sanger Harris remarks served to illustrate the
separate worlds in which local retailers and national
chains like Federated moved. In describing the managerial
revolution in American business, historian Alfred D.
Chandler, Jr., drew a similar parallel when comparing
businessmen of the 1840s with those of 1910. According to
Chandler, the former "would find the environment of

fifteenth century Italy more familiar than that of his own
nation seventy years later."[4] In like fashion, the independent retailers of Tucson could compare the dusty
cowtown of their business origins with the cosmopolitan
city which Federated now occupied. Jacome's and Tucson's
other retail establishments had their roots in an era when
local concerns dictated their survival. As a frontier
village far removed from the mainstream of American life,
Tucson had an economic environment which encouraged its
retailing community to look no further than the town's
borders. Internal concerns governed their activities, and
handcrafted methods of creating and maintaining their
clientele governed their days. At "La Bonanza," Carlos
completed a wide range of activities to maintain his store,
ranging from ordering the merchandise, to helping the
customers, to keeping the books, to participating in community activities. Governing his conduct throughout was
his personal integrity, a concern for honesty which ranked
at the same level of importance for his customers, the
townspeople, as the articles he sold.

Fundamental changes in American business organization and in the economy beginning before World War I and
reaching maturity during the 1920s, accompanied by a growing consumerism, had far-reaching effects on Carlos' world
and that of other Tucson retailers. The economic and
social forces producing these changes are complex and

varied, but among them were American expectations about an improved standard of living and a belief that new organizational forms would achieve these expectations. Also involved were two value shifts in American life: a new attitude toward spending characterized by a growing use of credit to buy an incessant stream of manufactured materials and a commitment to large rationalized structures to enable organizations efficiently to produce these materials. Accompanying organizational growth was the increasing power of corporate managers in American life. As national corporations moved into cities like Tucson, the arrival of these managers served to upset the old economic status balance within the local upper classes. Bringing with them the apparatus of the bureaucracies from which they emerged, these managers replaced the personalized services of the local entrepreneur with the impersonal and the automatized.[5] The story of Jacome's, in one sense then, becomes not one of a Mexican-American immigrant or entrepreneur but of a vanishing breed in American life, the small businessman.

These changes and the value shifts they brought benefitted local entrepreneurs in the short term, but in the long run they worked against their interests and brought their extinction. As consumerism grew in the 1920s, Jacome's joined the other retailers across the country in enjoying the advantages of the new expanding marketplace. More sophistication crept into their advertising, and a new awareness of markets beyond the city's boundaries caught management's imagination. Enjoying a virtual monopoly over Tucson's retail market, and then over the surrounding countryside as automobile use grew, Jacome's and their fellow merchants prospered and expanded from the end of World War II until the 1970s. Usually at the center of this new sensitivity to growing consumerism, however, was the recognition that they as merchants still owed much to the local community. As Carlos admonished his sons and employees, "Honesty, friendliness, and customer satisfaction," were still the hallmarks of the store.[6] Ultimately to adopt other policies would affect not only business but the integrity of the Jacome name. For this reason, the store resisted selling inferior merchandise, either through a bargain basement or at sale time.

Local entrepreneurs also enjoyed short-term benefits from the new management methods and procedures stimulating the growth of organizations nationwide. Structurally, for example, although Jacome's remained a simple organization with Carlos and then Alex retaining the role of final decision maker, the number of departments in the store multiplied. Growth in volume brought a system of merchandise control which in turn helped the store to expand even further.

The long-range effects of these new consumption patterns and large organizational growth on the local small businessman's survival was another matter. Rationalization brought an end to the folksy unsophisticated management style of an earlier era and paved the way for corporate forms of retail management more attuned to I.B.M. than small business. Consequently many problems emerged for the independent retailer. Some of the challenges beyond the control of even the best local management teams were a central city location, inadequate capital, a lack of scale economies, and unavailability of quantity discounts. Although independent department stores were some of the first to feel the effect of the chains and the changes wrought by rationalization, eventually even thriving specialty shops like Cele Peterson's and Dave Bloom and Sons faced possible extinction as the chain specialty stores began to penetrate the market. The small business person in Tucson had become the victim of what the economist Joseph Schumpeter described as the process of "creative destruction--the process by which private enterprise systems constantly create and destroy existing structures as a result of market forces."[7]

Yet, the once powerful and influential business families and institutions of Tucson have left their imprint upon the history and culture of the region they dominated. The mercantile families which guided Tucson's fortunes for several decades erected no concrete monuments for future generations to use and admire. No libraries, art museums, or concert halls bear their names. What does remain is an intangible, the memory of the downtown shopping area they created, an area which long served as a kind of social microcosm of the entire community. In the downtown atmosphere, both sales people and their customers were individuals with unique skills, talents, and needs. The family-controlled businesses--each creating its unique image through merchandise offerings, sales personnel, and store atmosphere--worked to satisfy the needs of the local community. Increasing complexity in the retailing environment brought to the fore the chain and its polarized labor force of deskilled sales people and professional managers. Downtown shopping came to an end, but the yearning for its return has lived on. Through the years, numerous newspaper and magazine articles continue to speculate about a rejuvenation of the downtown area.[8]

The imprint Jacome's left on downtown Tucson and the distinctive image the store conveyed to the community had deep roots in the cultural background of its founder. That the store survived and grew at a time when "nativism" contributed to a growing prejudice against Tucson's Mexican-Americans is a tribute to Carlos' ability to blend his culture with the larger community. His son, Alex, inherited his father's special talent for cultural blending, and it carried him into the "mainstream" of Tucson's economic and social life.

Culture also played an important role in the store's development of hemispheric and international trade with other Latin countries. That success makes doubly perplexing Sanger Harris Chairman Jack Miller's later remark that "Levy's would no longer cater its buying to the Mexican market, as Tucson's customers are looking for more traditional merchandise."[9] If, on the one hand, Miller was talking about potential Mexican customers among Tucson's population, despite the myriad changes in recent decades, the town's large Hispanic population had continued to grow. If, as seems more likely, the reference was directed toward the Mexican market south of the border, even the Arizona governor demonstrated a sensitivity toward commercial relations in the area, urging that "Mexico be made a higher U.S. priority."[10] Miller's remarks may have stemmed in part from the recognition that styles in clothing and home furnishings have become more homogeneous in the Western world in recent years. But they may also reflect the Southern traditions of Sanger Harris' home base in Dallas, very different from those of Tucson. While some awareness of the Hispanic borderlands exists in the West, the South, with the exception of New Orleans, apparently lacks this recognition.

In any case, Alex Jacome, Sr.'s development of U.S. trade with Latin America and Spain demonstrated for future generations the practical use that knowledge of Spanish-language skills and Latin culture and business practices can serve in carving out trade markets in Mexico, Spain, and other Latin countries. In particular, his approach to relations with Mexico gives him the appearance of a man ahead of his time, especially in today's world. Begun during the New Deal when Secretary of State Cordell Hull stressed economic rather than military ties with Latin America, Jacome's continued in the direction set by this Good Neighbor policy even when United States policy toward the region after World War II became one of general neglect.

Culturally, the Jacome store also provided an insight into the management style of Hispanics. Paramount in that style was an authoritarian decision-making mode and structure. More than in other retail establishments in downtown Tucson, family participation governed the store's operation throughout its history. Outside control, whether governmental or chain directed, was viewed in negative terms as an erosion of personal and family autonomy. The emphasis on hierarchical structures suggests several inter-esting and significant research possibilities. This is especially the case if, as some theorists predict, increas-ingly turbulent and unpredictable but interconnected environments will require greater efforts to manage them. These theorists hypothesize that changing conditions will bring an increasing concentration of power at the top of organizations, a continued emphasis on hierarchical author- ity, and bureaucratization of organizational roles and decision-making systems.[11]

It is to be hoped that our increased knowledge about Jacome's Department Store and the interplay of cul- ture and environment in its history will stimulate more research upon the relationship of minority cultures to business. The Jacome story demonstrates that culture can play a significant role in both the structure of an or- ganization and the survival strategy it chooses to pursue. Yet, it touches only the surface of minority cultural interaction with business life. Certainly the demographic explosion now taking place in Hispanic America, which is expected to accelerate as the country moves into the twenty-first century, will have a profound effect on busi- ness institutions. The implications of that impact reach far beyond economic considerations. In our competitive society where technology fuels the multiplication of goods, sources of energy, and services and where mobility paced by economic abundance encourages constant change and expecta- tion of increased rewards in the competitive struggle, business assumes a central role not only in reflecting but also in shaping the broader American culture.[12]

Chapter One

1. *Tucson Daily Citizen*, March, 24, 1929, p. 1; *Arizona Daily Star*, March 16, 1946, p. 14.

2. Howard R. Lamar, "Persistent Frontier: The West in the 20th Century," *Western Historical Quarterly*, Vol. IV, No. 1 (January 1973), p. 15.

3. Richard G. Arellano, *Strategies for Hispanic Business Development: Trends and Implications* (Washington, D.C.: National Chamber Foundation, 1984) pp. 1-5; *Time*, July 8, 1985, p. 26.

4. Several studies exist on the growth of the department store in the United States. Among these are anecdotal histories of particular firms or groups of firms which generally focus on personalities and managerial styles of the families who founded them. These include Margaret Case Harriman, *And The Price Is Right* (New York: The World Publishing Co., 1958), a study of Macy's; Mary La Dame, *The Filene Store* (New York: n.p., 1930); Boris Emmet and John E. Jeuck, *A History of Marshall Field and Co.* (Philadelphia: University of Pennsylvania Press, 1976); Maxine Brady, *Bloomingdales* (New York: Harcourt Brace and Jovanovich, 1980); and Herbert Adams Gibbons, *John Wanamaker* (New York: Harper and Brothers, 1926). Studies on the growth of the department store include John William Ferry, *A History of the Department Store* (New York: The Macmillan Company, 1960); Grant Pasdermadjian, *The Department Store: Its Origins, Evolution, and Economics* (New York: Arno Press, 1976); Robert Hendrickson, *The Grand Emporiums: The Illustrated History of America's Great Department Stores* (New York: Stein and Day, 1979); and Barry Bluestone et al., *The Retail Revolution: Market Transformation, Investment and Labor in the Modern Department Store* (Boston: Auburn House Publishing Co., 1981).

5. Robert H. Miles, *Macro Organizational Behavior* (Santa Monica, California: Goodyear Publishing, Inc., 1980), p. 190.

6. William R. Dill, "Environment as an Influence on Managerial Autonomy," *Administrative Science Quarterly*, Vol. 2 (March 1958), pp. 409-443.

7.   E. B. Tyler, *Primitive Culture*, 3rd English edition (London: John Murray Publishers, Ltd., 1891), p. 1, as cited in Frederick D. Sturdivant, *Business and Society: A Managerial Approach* (Homewood, Illinois: Richard D. Irwin, Inc., 1981), p. 27.

8.   Arellano, pp. 6-7.

9.   Rosaura Sanchez, "Chicano Bilingualism," in Ricardo Romo and Raymund Paredes (eds.) *New Directions in Chicano Scholarship* (San Diego: University of California, San Diego, 1978), p. 217.

10.   Americo Paredes, "On Ethnographic Work Among Minority Groups," in Romo and Paredes, *New Directions*, pp. 1-2; David Weber (ed.) *Foreigners in Their Native Land* (Albuquerque: University of New Mexico Press, 1973), p. 2.

11.   Michael V. Miller, "Variations in Mexican-American Family Life: A Review Synthesis of Empirical Research," *Aztlan*, Vol. 9 (Fall 1978), pp. 209-231.

12.   Allyn Gawain Spence, "Variables Contributing to the Maintenance of the Mexican-American Societal Structure in Tucson" (Unpublished masters thesis in Anthropology, University of Arizona, 1968), p. ix.

13.   John Dewey, *Democracy and Education* (New York: The Macmillan Co., 1916), pp. 10-11.

14.   Samuel Ramos as translated by Peter G. Earle, *Profile of Man and Culture in Mexico* (Austin: University of Texas Press, 1962), p. 26.

15.   Patrick Romanell, *Making of the Mexican Mind* (South Bend, Indiana, University of Notre Dame Press, 1967), pp. 13-66.

16.   Weber, pp. 59-61.

17.   Henry Steele Commager, *The American Mind: An Interpretation of American Thought and Character* (New Haven, Connecticut: Yale University Press, 1967), p. 18.

18.   Arellano, *Trends*, pp. 27-35.

19.   *Ibid*.

20.   *Ibid*.

21.   *Ibid*, p. 28.

22. *Ibid*, p. 29.

23. Arellano, *Strategies for Hispanic Business Development: Paths of Success, An Analysis of Case Studies* (Washington, D.C.: The National Chamber Foundation, 1984), p. 7.

24. Arellano, *Strategies for Hispanic Business Development: Agenda for Action, Recommendations* (Washington, D.C.: The National Chamber Foundation, 1984), pp. 5-7; *Arizona Daily Star*, July 9, 1984, Sec. A, p. 4.

25. *Ibid.*, p. 6.

26. Arellano, *Trends*, p. 31.

27. Weber, p. 4.

28. James Eoff Officer, "Sodalities and Systemic Linkage: The Joining Habits of Urban Mexican-Americans" (Unpublished doctoral dissertation in Anthropology, University of Arizona, 1964), pp. 72-74, 143-151.

29. Eugene Acosta Marin, "The Mexican-American Community and the Leadership of the Dominant Society" (Unpublished doctoral dissertation in Anthropology, University of Arizona, 1975), pp. 34-48.

30. *Tucson City Directory* (San Francisco: H. S. Crocker and Co., 1881), p. 2.

31. Joan Moore, *Mexican-Americans* (Englewood Cliffs, New Jersey: Prentice-Hall, Inc., 1970), p. 11.

32. Officer, "Sodalities," p. 50.

33. Officer, "Power in the Old Pueblo: A Study of Decision-Making," 1961 (Unpublished manuscript in The University of Arizona's Special Collections), p. 7.

34. Carey McWilliams, *North from Mexico: The Spanish-Speaking People in the United States* (New York: Greenwood Press, 1968), pp. 164-167.

35. Officer, "Historical Factors in Inter-Ethnic Relations in the Community of Tucson," *Arizoniana*, Vol. 1, No. 3 (Fall 1960), Arizona Heritage Center, Tucson.

36. Kaye Lynn Briegel, "Alianza Hispano-Americana, 1894-1965" (Unpublished doctoral dissertation in History, University of Southern California, 1974), pp. 22-26.

37. *Ibid.*; Marcy Gail Goldstein, "Americanization and Mexicanization: The Mexican Elite and Anglo-Americans in the Gadsden Purchase Lands, 1853-1880" (Unpublished doctoral dissertation in History, Case Western University, 1977), p. 308.

38. John Higham, *Strangers in the Land: Patterns of American Nativism, 1860-1925* (New York: Atheneum, 1963); Donald Kinzer, *An Episode in Anti-Catholicism: The American Protective Association* (Seattle: University of Washington Press, 1964), as cited in Briegel, p. 36.

39. "Alianza Hispano-Americana Observes Founder's Day Today" (Newspaper clipping, Arizona Heritage Center's clipping book, Tucson, Arizona).

40. Briegel, pp. 38-40.

41. *Ibid.*

42. *Tucson Daily Citizen*, September 15, 1907, pp. 8, 11, as cited in Officer, "Sodalities," p. 56.

43. *Ibid.*

44. Harry T. Getty, *Interethnic Relationships in the Community of Tucson* (New York: Arno Press, 1976), p. 195.

45. Joel D. Valdez Interview, June 21, 1984; Alex Jacome, Jr., Interview, February 13, 1984.

46. Officer, "Sodalities," p. 57.

47. Bicentennial Edition, *Arizona Daily Star*, August 24, 1975, Sec. D, p. 7.

48. Rodeo Edition, *Arizona Daily Star*, February 19, 1954, p. 2.

49. *Tucson Shopping Center Study: A Survey of Shopping Center Development and the Central Business District of Greater Tucson* (Phoenix: Research and Development of the First National Bank, June 1963), pp. 1-4.

50. *Tucson City Directory* (San Francisco: H. S. Crocker and Co., 1881), p. 13.

51. Officer, "Sodalities," p. 42.

52. *Ibid.*

53. *Ibid.*, p. 41.

54. Cele Peterson Interview, August 2, 1984; Herb Bloom Interview, June 20, 1984.

55. Getty, p. 113.

56. Pasdermadjian, pp. 3-5.

57. Bluestone et al., pp. 10-17.

58. *Ibid.*, p. 15.

59. *Ibid.*

Chapter Two

1. Thompson, *Organizations in Action* (New York: McGraw-Hill, 1967), pp. 27-28.

2. For a discussion of organizational culture see P. S. Cohen, "Theories of Myth," *Man*, Vol. 4, 1969, pp. 337-353; Andrew M. Pettigrew, "The Creation of Organizational Cultures," Paper presented to the Joint ELIASM-Dansk Management Center Research Seminar on Entrepreneurs and the Process of Institution Building, May 18-20, 1976, Copenhagen, as quoted in Miles, p. 48.

3. Miles, pp. 47-49.

4. *Tucson Daily Citizen*, December 9, 1932, p. 1; *Arizona Daily Star*, April 18, 1971; *Tucson Daily Citizen*, March 24, 1929, p. 1; *The Story of Jacomes, Being the Story of the Life of Carlos Jacome, Published on the Occassion (sic) of the 50th Anniversary of His Store*, Tucson, Arizona, March 18, 1946, Jacome File Special Collections, University of Arizona.

5. *Ibid.*, Alex Jacome, Jr., Interview, April 25, 1985.

6. *Tucson City Directory* (Tucson: Cobler and Co., 1883), p. 6.

7. *Ibid.*, 1881, p. 19.

8. Unpublished address to the Newcomen Society on March 11, 1965, by Alex Jacome, Sr. Manuscript in the possession of Professor Harwood Hinton who drafted it.

9. Don Bufkin, "The Broad Pattern of Land Use Change in Tucson, 1862-1912" in "Territorial Tucson," edited by Thomas F. Saarinen, M.S., p. 3, in possession of Don Bufkin, as quoted in C. L. Sonnichsen, *Tucson: The Life and Times of an American City* (Norman: The University of Oklahoma Press, 1982), p. 91; Bicentennial Edition, *Arizona Daily Star*, August 24, 1975, p. 10.

10. *Arizona Daily Star*, August 11, 1957, Sec. A, p. 6.

11. Dale Nichols, *The Story of Carlos Jacome* (Tucson: Pioneer Press, 1955), p. 3; *Tucson Daily Citizen*, March 24, 1929, p. 1.

12. *Arizona Daily Star*, August 25, 1957, Sec. A, p. 6.

13. *Ibid.*, August 11, 1957, Sec. A, p. 6; March 24, 1929, p. 1.

14. *Arizona Highways*, October 1950; *Tucson Daily Citizen*, January 23, 1954, p. 14; Sonnichsen, pp. 92-93.

15. Alex Jacome, Jr., Interview, February 13, 1984; *Tucson Daily Citizen*, December 9, 1932, p. 1; *Arizona Daily Star*, March 17, 1948, p. 5.

16. *Book of Marriages*, Pima County, May 18, 1891, p. 97, Carlos G. Jacome m. Dionisia Germán, filed June 3, 1891, by W. H. Calver, J.P.

17. *Tucson City Directory* (Tucson: Citizen Printing and Publishing Co., 1897-1898), p. 13.

18. *Ibid.*, 1899-1900, p. 16.

19. *Arizona Daily Star*, April 26, 1893.

20. *Ibid.*, August 11, 1957, Sec. A, p. 6; *Tucson Daily Citizen*, March 24, 1929, p. 1.

21. See, for example, Eric Hoffer, *The True Believer* (New York: Harper and Row, 1951), p. 45. Hoffer's theory is that immigrants are "temporary misfits" in their own country, the failures who hope to find success in a different place.

22. Arellano, *Trends*, p. 17.

23.   Officer, "Sodalities," pp. 73-74; Gordon Hewes, "Mexicans in Search of 'The Mexican,'" *American Journal of Economics and Sociology*, Vol. 13, No. 2 (January 1954), pp. 209-233; Verna Carleton Millan, *Mexico Reborn* (Boston: The Houghton Mifflin Co., 1939), p. 15.

24.   Lawrence A. Cardoso, *Mexican Emigration to the United States* (Tucson: The University of Arizona Press, 1980), p. 12.

25.   Ray Allen Billington (ed.), *The Frontier Thesis: Valid Interpretations of American History* (New York: Robert E. Kreege Publishing Co., 1977); Celestino Fernandez Interview, April 16, 1985; Weber, pp. 20-22.

26.   Arellano, *Paths*, pp. 7, 13, 20.

27.   Sonnichsen, pp. 53-55, 62, 84-85; James Eoff Officer, "Historical Factors in Interethnic Relations in the Community of Tucson," *Arizoniana*, Vol. 1 (Summer 1960), pp. 12-16.

28.   *Arizona Daily Star*, January 13, 1895, p. 4.

29.   *Ibid.*, August 11, 1957, Sec. A, p. 6.

30.   *Ibid.*, Hinton, Newcomen address.

31.   *Arizona Daily Star*, August 11, 1957, Sec. A, p. 6.

32.   Ferry, p. 4.

33.   Sonnichsen, p. 110.

34.   Eleventh Annual Rodeo Edition, *Arizona Daily Star*, February 22, 1935, p. 14.

35.   Sixteenth Annual Rodeo Edition, *Arizona Daily Star*, February 23, 1940, p. 3.

36.   *Arizona Daily Star*, January 31, 1952, Sec. B, p. 1.

37.   *Ibid.*

38.   John A. Henry and Cirino G. Scavone, "Cars Stop Here," *Smoke Signal, Tucson Corral of the Westerners* (Spring 1971), No. 23, p. 46; W. Eugene Caywood, *A History of Tucson Transportation* (Tucson: Pima County Historical Commission, n.d.), pp. 15-23; Eugene Caywood Interview, July 5, 1984.

39. *Arizona Daily Star*, July 27, 1969, Sec. C, p. 1.

40. *Ibid.*, January 16, 1896, p. 4; Eleventh Annual Rodeo Edition, February 22, 1935, p. 3; Sonnichsen, p. 133.

41. *Arizona Daily Star*, January 9, 1908, p. 2; Sonnichsen, p. 135.

42. *Ibid.*, Eleventh Annual Rodeo Edition, February 22, 1935, p. 3.

43. Arthur Stinchcombe, "Social Structure and Organizations," in *Handbook of Organizations*, edited by James G. March (Chicago: Rand-McNally, 1965), pp. 142-193.

44. Arellano, *Trends*, p. 31.

45. Augustine Jacome Interview, August 23, 1984.

46. Alex Jacome, Jr., Interview, February 13, 1984.

47. Thomas D. Clark, *Pills, Petticoats, and Plows: The Country Store* (Norman: The University of Oklahoma Press, 1964), passim; Herb Bloom Interview, June 20, 1984.

48. *Arizona Daily Star*, August 11, 1957, Sec. A, p. 6.

49. *Ibid.*, December 10, 1932, p. 1; December 11, 1932, p. 7.

50. *Ibid.*, August 11, 1957, Sec. A, p. 6.

51. Arellano, *Trends*, p. 31.

52. *Tucson Daily Citizen*, March 24, 1929, p. 1.

53. *Arizona Daily Star*, August 11, 1957, Sec. A, p. 6; September 8, 1957, Sec. A, p. 6.

54. Estela V. C. de Jacome Interview, August 9, 1984; *Arizona Daily Star*, August 11, 1957, Sec. A, p. 6. Alex Jacome, Jr., Interview, July 22, 1985.

55. *Arizona Daily Star*, August 25, 1957, Sec. A, p. 6.

56.   *Arizona Daily Star*, August 11, 1957, Sec. A, p. 6; *Tucson Daily Citizen*, March 24, 1929; Elisha P. Douglass, *The Coming of Age of American Business* (Chapel Hill: The University of North Carolina Press, 1971), p. 124; Boris Emmet and John E. Jeuck, *Catalogues and Counters: A History of Sears, Roebuck and Co.* (Chicago: University of Chicago, 1950), pp. 30-36; James C. Worth, *Shaping an American Institution* (Urbana: University of Illinois Press, 1984), p. 26.

57.   Clark, p. 32.

58.   *Arizona Daily Star*, August 11, 1957, Sec. A, p. 6.

59.   Jacome family private photo collection in possession of Estela V. C. de Jacome.

60.   Adelina Moreno Felix Interview, July 11, 1984.

61.   Ramona Figuero, 461 S. Myers St., sales slip, Jacome private papers in possession of Estela V. C. de Jacome.

62.   Augustine Jacome Interview, August 23, 1984.

63.   *Tucson Daily Citizen*, March 24, 1929, p. 1; *Arizona Daily Star*, August 25, 1957, Sec. A, p. 6.

64.   *Tucson Daily Citizen*, March 24, 1929, p. 1.

65.   *Ibid.*, Enriqueta Martinez DeMeester Interview, November 12, 1984.

66.   *Ibid.*

67.   *Tucson Daily Citizen*, February 20, 1954, p. 14; *Arizona Daily Star*, August 18, 1957, Sec. A, p. 6.

68.   *Arizona Daily Star*, August 18, 1957, Sec. A, p. 6.

69.   Arellano, *Trends*, pp. 27-29.

70.   *Tucson Daily Citizen*, March 24, 1929, p. 1.

71.   Elina Sayre Interview, October 2, 1984.

72.   *Arizona Daily Star*, September 8, 1957, Sec. A, p. 6; November 18-21, 1919, p. 1; *Tucson Daily Citizen*, February 12, 1904, p. 7.

73.   Sonnichsen, p. 170.

74.   *Tucson Daily Citizen*, April 8, 1913, pp. 1, 3.

75.   *Arizona Daily Star*, September 1, 1957, Sec. A, p. 6.

76.   Interviews with Herb Bloom, June 20, 1984; Ted Bloom, July 26, 1984; *Arizona Daily Star*, October 23, 1981, Sec. D, p. 1.

77.   Interviews with Dave Bloom, September 6, 1984; Herb Bloom, June 20, 1984.

78.   "In Old Tucson, 36 Years," *Arizona Daily Star*, March 24, 1946, p. 12; Maurice Horn (ed.), *The World Encyclopedia of Comics* (New York: Chelsea House, 1976), p. 145.

79.   Augustine Jacome Interview, August 23, 1984; Alex Jacome, Jr., Interview July 22, 1985.

80.   Ralph Beals, *No Frontiers to Learning* (Minneapolis: University of Minnesota Press, 1957) as quoted in Officer, "Sodalities," pp. 188-189.

81.   Elina Sayre Interview, October 2, 1984.

82.   *Tucson Daily Star*, April 6, 1984, p. 4.

83.   Pfeffer and Salancik, *The External Control of Organizations: A Resource Dependence Perspective* (New York: Harper and Row, 1976), p. 190.

84.   Officer, "Power," pp. 109-110; "In Old Tucson," *Arizona Daily Star*, November 12, 1925.

85.   Briegel, p. 40.

86.   *Ibid.*

87.   *Tucson Daily Citizen*, July 5, 1910, pp. 2, 4.

88.   *Tucson Daily Citizen*, August 8, 1910, p. 2; *Arizona Daily Star*, March 24, 1929, p. 1.

89.   *Ibid.*, August 10, 1910, p. 8; September 12, 1910, p. 1; September 13, 1910, p. 1.

90.   *Arizona Daily Star*, September 1, 1957, Sec. _, p. 1.

91. Ann Pace, "Mexican Refugees in Arizona, 1910-1911," *Arizona and the West*, Vol. XVI (Spring, 1974), pp. 5-18; Officer, "Factors," pp. 12-16.

92. *Tucson Daily Citizen*, June 22, 1920, p. 2; June 24, 1920, p. 3.

93. *Ibid.*, November 2, 1919, p. 2.

94. *Ibid.*, August 12, 1949, p. 3.

Chapter Three

1. *Recent Social Trends in the United States: Report of the President's Research Committee on Social Trends* (New York: McGraw-Hill, 1933), p. 867.

2. *Ibid.*

3. Franklin W. Ryan, "Family Finance in the U.S.," *Journal of Business of the University of Chicago*, Vol. III (October 1930), p. 417 as cited in *Recent Social Trends in the United States*, pp. 256-257.

4. Alex Jacome, Jr., Interview, June 7, 1984; April 25, 1985.

5. *Recent Economic Changes in the United States: Report of the Committee on Recent Economic Changes of the President's Conference on Unemployment* (New York: McGraw-Hill, 1929), Vol. II, p. 666.

6. Alex Jacome, Jr., Interview, June 7, 1984.

7. *Arizona Daily Star*, August 18, 1957, Sec. A, p. 6; February 11, 1921, pp. 2, 6.

8. *Ibid.*, August 18, 1957.

9. *Ibid.*

10. Enriqueta Martinez DeMeester Interview, November 12, 1984.

11. *Ibid.*

12. *Ibid.*

13. Alex Jacome, Jr., Interview, February 13, 1984.

14.   *Arizona Daily Star*, August 25, 1957, Sec. A, p. 6; *Tucson Daily Citizen*, August 12, 1949, p. 3; Augustine Jacome Interview, August 23, 1984.

15.   *Ibid.*

16.   *Arizona Daily Star*, August 25, 1957, Sec. A, p. 6.

17.   Enriqueta Martinez DeMeester Interview, November 12, 1984.

18.   *Recent Social Trends in the United States*, p. 880.

19.   *Arizona Daily Star*, August 24, 1957, Sec. A, p. 6.

20.   *Ibid.*

21.   *Tucson Daily Citizen*, March 24, 1929, p. 1.

22.   *Arizona Daily Star*, September 1, 1957, Sec. A, p. 6.

23.   *Tucson Daily Citizen*, March 24, 1929, p. 2.

24.   *Arizona Daily Star*, September 1, 1957, Sec. A, p. 6.

25.   *Index to Incorporations*, Pima County, Vol. 2, Jacome's Department Store, Inc., Articles of Incorporation, January 26, 1928, Vol. 13, pp. 384-387; *Tucson Daily Citizen*, October 27, 1929.

26.   Arellano, *Trends*, p. 28; *Paths*, p. 3.

27.   *Ibid.*

28.   Alfred D. Chandler, Jr., and Stephen Salsbury, *Pierre S. du Pont and the Making of the Modern Corporation* (New York: Harper and Row, 1971), p. 592.

29.   *Ibid.*

30.   *Ibid.*, pp. 591-604.   See also Alfred D. Chandler, Jr., *The Visible Hand: The Managerial Revolution in American Business* (Cambridge, Massachusetts: The Belknap Press of Harvard University Press, 1977), pp. 438-450; Alfred D. Chandler, Jr., *Strategy and Structure* (New York: Doubleday, 1962), passim.

31. *Ibid.*

32. Alfred D. Chandler, Jr., and Stephen Salsbury, *Pierre S. du Pont*, pp. 48, 644.

33. *Ibid.*, pp. 137, 591-604.

34. Alex Jacome, Jr., Interview, June 7, 1984.

35. *Arizona Daily Star*, March 17, 1948, p. 5; *Tucson Daily Citizen*, August 12, 1949, p. 3.

36. Augustine Jacome Interview, August 23, 1984.

37. *Arizona Daily Star*, September 1, 1957, Sec. A, p. 6.

38. Julie A. Matthaei, *An Economic History of Women in America: Women's Work, the Sexual Division of Labor and the Development of Capitalism* (New York: Schocken Books, 1982), pp. 30-32.

39. *Arizona Daily Star*, September 1, 1957, Sec. A, p. 6.

40. Elina Sayre Interview, October 2, 1984.

41. *Tucson Daily Citizen*, March 24, 1929, p. 1; April 20, 1929, pp. 1-2.

42. *Ibid.*

43. *Tucson Daily Citizen*, September 30, 1928, p. 1; *Arizona Daily Star*, December 12, 1929, p. 1; April 20, 1929, p. 1.

44. *Ibid.*, June 25, 1959; "Jacome Returns from Vacation," (Newspaper clipping, Arizona Heritage Center's clipping book, Tucson, Arizona).

45. "Albert Steinfeld is Back: Veteran Businessman Back from New York Where He Saw Sun Shine But Once," (Newspaper clipping, Arizona Heritage Center's clipping book, Tucson, Arizona).

46. Pasdermadjian, pp. 49-53.

47. *Tucson City Directory* (Los Angeles: Arizona Directory Co., 1913), p. 83; *Tucson City Directory* (Tucson: Western Directory Co., 1921), p. 201; Bicentennial Edition, *Arizona Daily Star*, August 24, 1975, Sec. D, p. 11.

48. Herb Bloom Interview, June 20, 1984.

49. Cele Peterson Interview, August 1, 1984.

50. Levy's Scrapbook, "Memoirs of Leon Levy," *Arizona Daily Star*, April 21, 1948; June 14, 1931, p. 5; Leon Levy Interview, November 5, 1984.

51. Estela V. C. de Jacome Interview, August 9, 1984; Enriqueta Martinez DeMeester Interview, November 12, 1984; John Bret Harte, *Tucson: Portrait of a Desert Pueblo* (Woodland Hills, California: Windsor Publications, 1980), p. 90.

52. Richard A. Cosgrove, "Regionalism and Localism in Patterns of Mexican-American Discrimination: The Tucson Evidence." Unpublished paper in possession of Professor Cosgrove, pp. 19, 27.

53. Getty, pp. 140-150.

54. *Tucson Daily Citizen*, November 24, 1929, p. 7.

55. *Arizona Daily Star*, August 18, 1957, Sec. A, p. 1.

56. *Ibid.*, March 16, 1946, p. 14.

57. *Ibid.*, August 18, 1957, Sec. A, p. 6.

58. *Ibid.*, September 8, 1957, Sec. A, p. 6.

59. *Arizona Daily Star*, September 8, 1958, Sec. A, p. 6.

60. *Ibid.*

61. Augustine Jacome Interview, August 23, 1984; *Tucson Daily Citizen*, June 13, 1931; June 14, 1931.

62. *Arizona Daily Star*, August 18, 1957, Sec. A, p. 6; Enriqueta Martinez DeMeester Interview, November 12, 1984; *Arizona Daily Star*, September 4, 1925, p. 3.

63. Augustine Jacome Interview, August 23, 1984.

64. *Tucson Daily Citizen*, December 10, 1932, p. 1; *Arizona Daily Star*, December 10, 1932, p. 1; December 11, 1932, p. 7.

Chapter Four

1.   Arellano, *Trends*, p. 31.

2.   Neal Juston, "Mexican-American Achievement Hindered by Cultural Conflict," *Sociology and Social Research* (July 1972), pp. 471-486; Spence, pp. 54-58; Arellano, *Trends*, p. 7.

3.   Alex Jacome, Jr., Interview, February 13, 1984; Augustine Jacome Interview, August 30, 1984; *Arizona Daily Star*, March 17, 1948, p. 5; Adelina Moreno Felix Interview, July 11, 1984.

4.   Hinton, Newcomen address; Augustine Jacome Interview, August 30, 1984; Estela V. C. de Jacome Interview, August 9, 1984.

5.   Pfeffer and Salancik, pp. 236-238.

6.   Alex Jacome, Jr., Interview, February 13, 1984.

7.   *Ibid.*

8.   Thomas C. Cochran, *The Puerto Rican Businessman* (Philadelphia: University of Pennsylvania Press, 1959), pp. 123-127.

9.   Alex Jacome, Jr., Interview, February 13, 1984; Augustine Jacome Interview, August 30, 1984.

10. Arellano, *Trends*, p. 8.

11. Interviews with Holden Olsen, August 7, 1984; Gail Hummel, July 5, 1984; Alex Jacome, Jr., June 7, 1984; Sam McMillan, June 20, 1984; and Adelina Moreno Felix, July 11, 1984.

12. Juston, pp. 471-486.

13. Enriqueta Martinez DeMeester Interview, November 12, 1984; "Ole," *Tucson Daily Citizen*, May 27, 1972, p. 9.

14. *Ibid.*

15. Enriqueta Martinez DeMeester Interview, November 12, 1984.

16. *Arizona Daily Star*, July 17, 1934, Sec. 2, p. 1.

17. Enriqueta Martinez DeMeester Interview, November 12, 1984; Jim Davis Interview, August 30, 1984; Hinton, Newcomen address.

18. *Arizona Daily Star*, March 17, 1948; Hinton, Newcomen address.

19. Pasdermadjian, p. 54.

20. William H. Jervey, Jr., "When the Banks Closed," *Arizona and the West*, Vol. 10 (Summer 1968), p. 143.

21. "NRA is Working Jacome States." (Newspaper clipping, Arizona Heritage Center's clipping book, Tucson, Arizona).

22. Barton J. Bernstein, "The New Deal: The Conservative Achievements of Liberal Reform," *Toward a New Past: Dissenting Essays in American History* (New York: Pantheon Books, 1968), pp. 263-288.

23. "NRA is Working Jacome States." (Newspaper clipping, Arizona Heritage Center's clipping book, Tucson, Arizona).

24. Bluestone et al., *The Retail Revolution*, pp. 120-133; Burton A. Zorn and George J. Felman, *Business Under the New Price Laws: A Study of the Economic and Legal Problems Arising Out of the Robinson-Patman Act and the Various Fair Trade and Unfair Practices Laws* (New York: Prentice Hall, 1937), pp. xi, 126-127.

25. *Ibid.*; L. Louise Luchsinger and Patrick M. Dunne, "Fair Trade Laws--How Fair?," *Journal of Marketing* (Worcester, Massachusetts: Hefferman Press, Inc., 1978), pp. 50-53; Bruce J. Walker, "Arizona Retailers on Fair Trade Repeal," *Arizona Business*, Vol. XXIII, No. 2 (Arizona State University: Bureau of Business and Economic Research, 1975), pp. 20-28.

26. Mildred C. Devine, "An Evaluation of the Methods of Merchandise Control." (Unpublished master's thesis in Education, University of Arizona, 1959), passim.

27. Enriqueta Martinez DeMeester Interview, November 12, 1984.

28. Alex Jacome, Jr., Interview, June 7, 1984; Enriqueta Martinez DeMeester Interview, November 12, 1984.

29. *Arizona Daily Star*, December 25, 1941, p. 2.

30. *Tucson Daily Citizen*, March 16, 1946, p. 14; Alex Jacome, Jr., Interview, July 16, 1985.

31. *Arizona Daily Star*, January 22, 1933, p. 2.

32. Officer, "Sodalities," p. 61.

33. Sonnichsen, pp. 243-244.

34. Leo Grebler et al., *The Mexican-American People: The Nation's Second Largest Minority* (New York: The Free Press, 1970), pp. 66, 523-526; Sonnichsen, p. 238; Briegel, p. 113.

35. Robert Divine, *American Immigration Policy, 1924-1952* (New Haven: Yale University Press, 1957), pp. 252-266.

36. "Alex G. Jacome," February 27, 1959, Jacome File, Special Collections, The University of Arizona; Cele Peterson Interview, August 2, 1984.

37. *Ibid.*

38. Harwood Hinton Interview, June 28, 1984.

39. Enriqueta Martinez DeMeester Interview, November 12, 1984; Introduction of Mr. Alex G. Jacome by Richard Harvill, President of The University of Arizona to the Newcomen Society, March 11, 1965, Jacome private papers in possession of Estela V. C. de Jacome.

40. "Ole," *Tucson Daily Citizen*, May 27, 1972, p. 9.

41. *Nogales Arizona International*, September 22, 1976, p. 10; "Alex G. Jacome," Jacome File, Special Collections, The University of Arizona.

42. *Arizona Daily Star*, September 8, 1957, Sec. A, p. 1.

43. "Alex G. Jacome," February 27, 1959, Jacome File, Special Collections, The University of Arizona.

44. Hinton, Newcomen address: "Alex G. Jacome," February 27, 1959, Jacome File, Special Collections, The University of Arizona; Holden Olsen Interview, August 7, 1984.

45. Enriqueta Martinez DeMeester Interview, November 12, 1984; Jim Davis Interview, August 30, 1984.

46.   "Jacome's Has Oldest Shoes."   (Newspaper clipping, Arizona Heritage Center's clipping book, Tucson, Arizona).

47.   *Tucson Daily Citizen*, September 11, 1941, p. 8.

48.   *Tucson Daily Citizen*, December 6, 1945, p. 4; Helen Middleton Interview, July 29, 1985; Richard Barcels Interview, July 30, 1985; *Tucsotarian*, December 5, 1945; December 12, 1945; May 8, 1946.

49.   Hinton, Newcomen address: *Tucson Daily Citizen*, May 27, 1972, p. 9; *Arizona Daily Star*, January 1, 1944, p. 5; January 9, 1944, p. 1; Alex Jacome, Jr., Interview, July 22, 1985.

50.   Harry T. Getty, *Interethnic Relationships in the Community of Tucson* (Doctoral Dissertation Microfilm, University of Chicago, 1950), pp. 238-240.

51.   Augustine Jacome Interview, August 23, 1984; *Tucson Daily Citizen*, June 16, 1944; March 2, 1944.

52.   *Arizona Daily Star*, October 6, 1945, p. 9.

53.   Estela V. C. de Jacome Interview, August 9, 1984.

54.   "Celebrate Shoes Anniversary."   (Newspaper clipping, Arizona Heritage Center's clipping book, Tucson, Arizona).

55.   *Arizona Daily Star*, August 17, 1950, p. 1.

56.   *Tucson Daily Citizen*, January 17, 1980, p. 1e.

57.   *Arizona Daily Star*, March 16, 1946, p. 14.

58.   *Ibid.*

59.   *Ibid.*

60.   *Ibid.*, October 6, 1945, p. 5; Levy's Section, September 14, 1969, p. 2; Levy's Scrapbook, "Memoirs of Leon Levy."

61.   Herb Bloom Interview, June 20, 1984.

62.   *Arizona Daily Star*, August 17, 1950, p. 1.

63. Henry and Scavone, pp. 46-64; Caywood, *pp. 15-23; W. Eugene Caywood Interview, July 5, 1984.*

64. *Tucson Daily Citizen,* July 13, 1939, p. 1; April 9, 1946, p. 1.

65. Leon Levy Interview, November 5, 1984.

66. Levy's Scrapbook, "Memoirs of Leon Levy."

67. Bret Harte, p. 340; Eugene Hollon, *The South-west: Old and New* (New York: Alfred A. Knopf, 1961), p. 444.

68. Pasdermadjian, pp. 71-72; Augustine Jacome Interview, August 30, 1984.

69. Bluestone et al., pp. 15-18.

70. *Ibid.*

Chapter Five

1. *The Wall Street Journal,* August 21, 1950, p. 5.

2. *Time,* August 28, 1950.

3. Bluestone et al., p. 46.

4. Harold G. Vatter, *The U.S. Economy in the 1950's: An Economic History* (New York: W. W. Norton and Co., 1963), pp. 93-94, 116.

5. Sonnichsen, p. 283.

6. Harte, p. 138.

7. *Women's Wear Daily,* September 12, 1951; West-brook Pegler, *The Los Angeles Examiner,* September 12, 1951.

8. Jacome private papers in the possession of Estela V. C. de Jacome.

9. Estela V. C. de Jacome Interview, August 9, 1984.

10. Sam McMillan Interview, June 20, 1981; Holden Olsen Interview, August 7, 1984.

11. *Arizona Daily Star*, September 2, 1951, Sec. A, p. 1; September 9, 1951, Sec. B, p. 1.

12. Alex Jacome, Jr., Interview, February 13, 1984; Jim Davis Interview, August 30, 1984.

13. "Dick" of Society Brand Clothes to Alex Jacome, August 21, 1950, Jacome private papers in the possession of Estela V. C. de Jacome.

14. *Arizona Daily Star*, September 9, 1951, Sec. B, p. 1.

15. *Ibid.*, September 9, 1951, p. 3.

16. Alex Jacome, Jr., Interview, July 22, 1985.

17. Hinton, Newcomen address.

18. *Arizona Daily Star*, September 9, 1951, Sec. B, p. 1.

19. Jacome private papers in the possession of Estela V. C. de Jacome.

20. *Ibid.*

21. *Ibid.*

22. *Arizona Daily Star*, October 28, 1954.

23. *Ibid.*, September 9, 1951, p. 1; Toleta Martinez Interview, August 7, 1985.

24. Fred I. Steele, *Physical Settings and Organizational Development* (Reading, Massachusetts: Addison-Wesley, 1973), p. 38; Alex Jacome, Jr., Interview, July 22, 1985.

25. Enriqueta Martinez DeMeester Interview, November 19, 1984; Alex Jacome, Sr., to Fred Emery, telephone call recorded by Emery's secretary at 11:00 p.m. on November 19, 1954, and in possession of Mrs. Fred Emery.

26. Alex G. Jacome to Robert Fish, Los Altos, California, September 19, 1957, Uncatalogued Jacome papers hereafter referred to as (J.P.) Special Collections, The University of Arizona; Getty, p. 143.

27. Officer, "Power," pp. 144-145.

28. *Ibid.*

29.   *Arizona Daily Star*, March 25, 1982, Sec. C, p. 1.

30.   Greber et al., p. 279.

31.   Arellano, *Trends*, p. 13.

32.   *Arizona Daily Star*, March 17, 1948, p. 5; April 24, 1954, Sec. B, p. 8; *Tucson Daily Citizen*, January 17, 1980; Officer, "Sodalities," p. iii.

33.   Hinton, Newcomen address; *Arizona Daily Star*, July 27, 1954, p. 1; July 30, 1943, p. 8; August 22, 1954, Sec. C, p. 8; September 14, 1954, Sec. B, pp. 1-2; September 17, 1954, Sec. C, p. 5.

34.   *Ibid*.

35.   *Ibid*.

36.   Barry Goldwater to The Honorable Robert Hill, Ambassador Extraordinary and Plenipotentiary, U.S. Embassy, Mexico City, D. F., August 21, 1957 (J.P.) Special Collections, The University of Arizona.

37.   *Arizona Daily Star*, May 24, 1959, p. 1; Alex Jacome, Jr., Interview, July 22, 1985; Jacome Department Store Christmas card, 1959, in possession of Alex Jacome, Jr.

38.   *Ibid*.

39.   D. H. Steele, Hamilton Advertising Agency, to Alex G. Jacome, August 23, 1950 (J.P.) Special Collections, The University of Arizona.

40.   Estela V. C. de Jacome Interview, August 9, 1984; Grace Bourguignon Interview, July 31, 1984.

41.   Arellano, *Trends*, p. 10.

42.   Estela V. C. de Jacome Interview, August 9, 1984; Rosabeth Moss Kanter, *Men and Women of the Corporation* (New York: Basic Books, Inc., 1977), pp. 119-120.

43.   *Ibid*.

44.   La Paz, Bolivia, trip clipping, Jacome private papers in possession of Estela V. C. de Jacome.

45.   Estela V. C. de Jacome Interview, August 9, 1984.

46. C. Wright Mills, *White Collar: The American Middle Classes* (New York: Oxford University Press, 1953), p. 165; Bluestone et al., pp. 2-4; Grace Bourguignon Interview, July 31, 1984.

47. Edna Dillon to Alex G. Jacome, August 31, 1950 (J.P.) Special Collections, The University of Arizona; Mills, *White Collar*, p. 173.

48. Interviews with Grace Bourguignon, July 31, 1984; Enriqueta Martinez DeMeester, November 19, 1984; Librado (Tony) Anton, July 24, 1984; and Toleta Martinez, August 7, 1984.

49. Toleta Martinez Interview, August 8, 1984.

50. Grace Bourguignon Interview, July 31, 1984.

51. Interviews with Grace Bourguignon, July 31, 1984; Enriqueta Martinez DeMeester, November 19, 1984; Librado (Tony) Anton, July 24, 1984; and Toleta Martinez, August 7, 1984.

52. *Ibid.*

53. *Arizona Daily Star*, September 8, 1957, Sec. A, p. 6.

54. Librado (Tony) Anton Interview, July 24, 1984.

55. Enriqueta Martinez DeMeester Interview, November 19, 1984.

56. Pasdermadjian, p. 64; Mills, *White Collar*, p. 180.

57. Alex Jacome, Jr., Interview, June 7, 1984.

58. Devine, p. 13; Alex G. Jacome to Ralph Nader, June 14, 1976 (J.P.) Special Collections, The University of Arizona.

59. Devine, pp. 4, 31.

60. *Ibid.*, p. 51.

61. *Ibid.*, p. 39.

62. *Ibid.*, p. 14.

63. Alex Jacome, Jr., Interview, June 7, 1984; Devine, p. 14.

64. *Ibid.*

65. *Arizona Daily Star*, September 9, 1951, p. 1.

66. Tucson Chamber of Commerce, *Outlook*, October 2, 1979, p. 2.

67. *Women's Wear Daily*, December 26, 1951.

68. *Arizona Daily Star*, December 14, 1951.

69. Letters (J.P.) Special Collections, The University of Arizona.

70. Devine, p. 42; Mills, *White Collar*, p. 164.

71. Devine, pp. 42, 47.

72. Alex Jacome, Jr., Interview, June 8, 1984.

73. *Arizona Daily Star*, August 25, 1957, Sec. A, p. 6.

74. Devine, p. 7.

75. *Ibid.*, p. 49.

76. *Ibid.*, p. 6.

77. *Ibid.*, pp. 15-16.

78. *Ibid.*, p. 17.

79. *Arizona Daily Star*, September 8, 1957, Sec. B, pp. 11-12; *Tucson Daily Citizen*, April 16, 1956.

80. *Arizona Daily Star*, August 25, 1957, Sec. A, p. 1.

81. *Ibid.*, August 11, 18, 25, 1957; September 1, 8, 1957, Sec. A, p. 6.

82. A. G. Jacome to Mr. John Burnham, Experiment Station Editor, College of Agriculture and Agricultural Experiment Station, The University of Arizona, August 14, 1957 (J.P.) Special Collections, The University of Arizona.

83. A. G. Jacome to Westbrook Pegler, September 4, 1957 (J.P.) Special Collections, The University of Arizona.

84. *Ibid.*; Oliver Pilat, *Pegler: Angry Man of the Press* (Boston: Beacon Press, 1963), pp. 51, 110-111, 188.

85. Daniel W. Raaf, "Downtown Tucson and the Woman Shopper," *Arizona Business and Economic Review*, Vol. 7, No. 4 (April, 1958), p. 8.

86. *Tucson Trade Bureau Analysis of Downtown* (Los Angeles: Developmental Research Association, 1969), p. 7.

87. Nathan and Flo Kaiserman Interviews, May 21, 1985.

88. *Arizona Daily Star*, January 4, 1953, p. 1; Fred Emery, "A City in Action, 1951-1954: Four Years of Progress," City of Tucson, Office of the Mayor, in possession of Mrs. Fred Emery.

89. *Arizona Daily Star*, January 6, 1953, p. 4.

90. *Ibid.*, January 10, 1953, p. 9; January 20, 1953, p. 1.

91. *Arizona Daily Star*, Progress Editions, February 5, 1945, April 6, 1957.

92. *Ibid.*, August 6, 1954, p. 3.

93. *Ibid.*, February 15, 1956, Sec. B, p. 1; January 6, 1956, p. 6.

94. Leon Levy Interview, November 5, 1984.

95. Gene Caywood Interview, July 5, 1984.

96. *Arizona Daily Star*, July 30, 1955, Sec. B, p. 1.

97. Levy's Scrapbook, "Memoirs of Leon Levy."

98. *Arizona Daily Star*, September 20, 1958, Sec. B, p. 1.

99. Herb Bloom Interview, June 20, 1984.

100. Peter Johnson Interview, July 5, 1984; Leon Levy Interview, November 5, 1984.

101. Mills, *White Collar*, p. 50.

Chapter Six

1. Howard E. Morgan, "The Changing Structure of the Distributive Trades in Arizona," Part II, *Arizona Review*, Vol. 9, No. 3 (March 1960), pp. 1-23.

2.   Officer, "Power," p. 61; Mills, *The Power Elite* (New York: Oxford University Press, 1956), pp. 12, 19, 36-39, 43.

3.   Leon Levy Interview, November 5, 1984.

4.   *Ibid.*, p. 71.

5.   Leon Levy Interview, November 5, 1984.

6.   Alex G. Jacome to Lee Davis, August 2, 1965 (J.P.) Special Collections, The University of Arizona.

7.   Alex G. Jacome to Mayor Lew Davis and City Councilmen, April 7, 1967 (J.P.) Special Collections, The University of Arizona.

8.   Alex G. Jacome to Senators Frank Felix, Douglas Holsclaw, Carmen Cajero, November 21, 1973 (J.P.) Special Collections, The University of Arizona.

9.   Arellano, *Trends*, p. 32.

10.   Edward Kirkland, *Dream and Thought in the Business Community, 1860-1900* (Ithaca, New York: Cornell University Press, 1956), pp. 13-20; Mills, *White Collar*, pp. 36, 57.

11.   Alex G. Jacome, "Address to the Tucson Women's Club," 1963 (J.P.) Special Collections, The University of Arizona.

12.   Greber et al., pp. 6, 532; Senator Dennis DeConcini to Alex G. Jacome, July 13, 1979 (J.P.) Special Collections, The University of Arizona.

13.   Alex G. Jacome to Honorable Paul Fannin, March 17, 1970 (J.P.) Special Collections, The University of Arizona; Arellano, *Agenda*, p. 16.

14.   Alex G. Jacome, "Letters to the Editor," *Arizona Daily Star*, April 29, 1970, Sec. D, p. 14.

15.   Alex G. Jacome to Honorable Paul Fannin, May 7, 1975 (J.P.) Special Collections, The University of Arizona.

16.   Alex G. Jacome to Dr. Paul Rosenblatt, November 4, 1976 (J.P.) Special Collections, The University of Arizona.

17.   Alex G. Jacome to Senator Paul Fannin, March 17, 1970 (J.P.) Special Collections, The University of Arizona.

18.   Alex F. Jacome, Jr., Interview, June 8, 1984; Nina Avennenti Interview, May 21, 1985.

20.   Alex G. Jacome to Helen D. Seright, October 17, 1969 (J.P.) Special Collections, The University of Arizona.

21.   Alex G. Jacome, "Letters to the Editor," *Arizona Daily Star*, December 21, 1966, p. 22.

22.   Mrs. Frank D. Wilkey to Alex G. Jacome, January 16, 1967 (J.P.) Special Collections, The University of Arizona.

23.   Alex G. Jacome to Lucille S. Abel, May 15, 1976 (J.P.) Special Collections, The University of Arizona.

24.   Alex Jacome, Jr., Interview, June 7, 1984.

25.   Alex G. Jacome to Senator Barry Goldwater, March 27, 1962; Barry Goldwater to Alex G. Jacome, April 9, 1963 (J.P.) Special Collections, The University of Arizona.

26.   Ferry, pp. 40, 54, 66, 170.

27.   Bluestone et al., pp. 3, 17, 144.

28.   Henry Quinto Interview, January 11, 1984; Leon Levy Interview, November 4, 1984.

29.   *Arizona Daily Star*, November 5, 1962.

30.   *Ibid.*, February 5, 1965.

31.   *Tucson Daily Citizen*, November 29, 1967, p. 37.

32.   *Arizona Daily Star*, April 6, 1972, Sec. D, p. 7.

33.   Gilbert Martinez to Alex G. Jacome, April 26, 1968 (J.P.) Special Collections, The University of Arizona.

34.   See for example *El Sonorense*, Hermosillo, Sonora, April 24, 1958; *Nogales Arizona International*, September 22, 1976.

35.   *Department Store Journal* (April 1964), pp. 51-52.

36.   Jacome Department Store to Dr. E. L. Larson, February 11, 1962 (J.P.) Special Collections, The University of Arizona.

37.   *Arizona Daily Star*, December 4, 1978, Sec. D, p. 4; Jacome Flyer, "Gilberto A. Jacome Memorial Day Special Opening for the Handicapped" (J.P.) Special Collections, The University of Arizona.

38.   *Tucson Daily Citizen*, September 27, 1967, p. 1.

39.   *Arizona Daily Star*, March 4, 1928; Alex Jacome, Jr., Interview, July 22, 1985).

40.   Mary Hamm Spencer to Jacome's Department Store, October 16, 1969 (J.P.) Special Collections, The University of Arizona.

41.   Henry Quinto Interview, January 11, 1984.

42.   Herb Bloom Interview, June 20, 1984.

43.   Alex G. Jacome to Mary Hamm Spencer, October 17, 1967 (J.P.) Special Collections, The University of Arizona.

44.   Jim Davis Interview, August 30, 1984.

45.   Alex Jacome, Jr., Interview, February 13, 1984.

46.   Holden Olsen Interview, August 7, 1984.

47.   Alex Jacome, Jr., Interview, February 13, 1984; *Arizona Daily Star*, January 23, 1958, p. 1; July 20, 1958, Sec. B, p. 1.

48.   Levy's Scrapbook, "Memoirs of Leon Levy;" *Arizona Daily Star*, August 31, 1969, Sec. C, p. 11; "Levy's Section," September 14, 1969.

49.   Henry Quinto Interview, January 11, 1984.

50.   Levy's Scrapbook, "Memoirs of Leon Levy;" *Arizona Daily Star*, September 7, 1969, Sec. A, p. 8.

51.   *Tucson Daily Citizen*, March 17, 1969, p. 43.

52. "Retail Scene Tucson," *Daily News Record*, August 3, 1972.

53. *Arizona Daily Star*, December 23, 1979, Sec. D, p. 1.

54. Cele Peterson Interview, August 2, 1984.

55. *Ibid.*

56. *Arizona Daily Star*, December 20, 1970, p. 1; *Tucson Daily Citizen*, January 15, 1971.

57. Cele Peterson Interview, August 2, 1984.

58. *Arizona Daily Star*, September 19, 1976, Sec. H, p. 1.

59. Bluestone et al., pp. 120-131; Luchsinger and Dunne, p. 53; Walker, pp. 20-27.

60. Interview with Nathan and Flo Kaiserman, May 21, 1985; Jim Davis Interview, August 30, 1984.

61. "Retail Scene Tucson," *Daily News Record*, August 3, 1972.

62. *Arizona Daily Star*, March 27, 1971, p. 15; March 28, 1971, Sec. C, p. 1.

63. Cele Peterson Interview, August 2, 1984; *Arizona Daily Star*, November 9, 1979, p. 1.

64. *Arizona Daily Star*, May 29, 1976, Sec. E, p. 9.

65. Alex Jacome, Jr., Interview, February 13, 1984; *Arizona Daily Star*, May 29, 1976, Sec. E, p. 9; February 22, 1978, p. 6.

66. Alex Jacome, Jr., Interview, February 13, 1984; Sam McMillan Interview, June 20, 1984.

67. Bluestone et al., pp. 25, 63, 67; Alex Jacome, Jr., Interview, February 13, 1984.

68. Alex Jacome, Jr., Interview, February 13, 1984.

69. Greber et al., pp. 350-351; Alex F. Jacome, Jr., Interview, February 13, 1984.

70.   Alex Jacome, Jr., Interview, February 13, 1984.

71.   *Tucson Daily Citizen*, January 17, 1980, p. 1.

72.   *Arizona Daily Star*, January 15, 1980, p. 1.

73.   *Tucson Daily Citizen*, January 17, 1980, p. 1.

74.   *Ibid.*, January 15, 1980, p. 1.

75.   *Ibid.*, January 17, 1980, p. 1.

76.   *Arizona Daily Star*, January 15, 1980, p. 1.

77.   *The Arizona Alumnus*, April 1980.

78.   *Arizona Daily Star*, March 6, 1980, p. 3.

79.   Grace Bourguignon Interview, July 31, 1984; Librado (Tony) Anton Interview, July 24, 1984; Nina Avennenti Interview, May 21, 1985.

80.   Grace Bourguignon Interview, July 31, 1984.

81.   *Arizona Daily Star*, April 3, 1980, Sec. B, p. 1.

82.   Nina Avennenti Interview, May 21, 1985.

83.   *Arizona Daily Star*, April 3, 1980, Sec. B, p. 1.

84.   Leon Levy Interview, November 7, 1984.

85.   Librado (Tony) Anton Interview, July 24, 1984.

86.   Grace Bourguignon Interview, July 31, 1984; Toleta Martinez Interview, August 7, 1984.

87.   Grace Bourguignon Interview, July 31, 1984.

88.   *Tucson Daily Citizen*, April 5, 1980, Sec. B, p. 1.

89.   *Ibid.*

Chapter Seven

1.   *Arizona Daily Star*, October 4, 1984, Sec. F, p. 1; October 13, 1984, Sec. D, p. 9.

2.   *Ibid.*

3.   *Ibid.*, May 17, 1985, p. 1.

4.   Chandler, *The Visible Hand*, p. 455.

5.   William G. Scott, *Organizational Theory: A Structural and Behavioral Analysis* (Homewood, Illinois: Richard D. Irwin, Inc., 1983), p. 333; Joseph Schumpeter, *Capitalism, Socialism, and Democracy*, 3rd ed. (New York: Harper and Row, 1942), pp. 131-142.

6.   *Tucson Daily Citizen*, March 24, 1929, p. 1.

7.   Schumpeter, pp. 81-86 as quoted in Bluestone et al., p. 139.

8.   See for example *Arizona Daily Star*, March 24, 1985.

9.   *Arizona Daily Star*, May 17, 1985, p. 1.

10.   *Ibid*, June 21, 1985.

11.   Pfeffer and Salancik, pp. 282-285.

12.   David M. Potter, *People of Plenty: Economic Abundance and the American Character* (Chicago: The University of Chicago Press, 1954), passim.

LIST OF REFERENCES

INTERVIEWS

Anton, Librado (Tony), July 24, 1984.

Avennenti, Nina, June 8, 1984.

Barcelo, Richard, July 30, 1985.

Bloom, Dave, August 23, 1984; September 6, 1984.

Bloom, Herb, June 20, 1984.

Bloom, Ted, July 26, 1984.

Bourguignon, Grace, July 31, 1984.

Caywood, Eugene, July 5, 1984.

Davis, Jim, August 30, 1984.

DeMeester, Enriqueta Martinez, November 12, 1984; November 19, 1984.

Felix, Adelina Moreno, July 11, 1983.

Fernandez, Celestino, April 16, 1985.

Harvill, Richard, June 28, 1984.

Hinton, Harwood, June 28, 1984.

Hummel, Gail, July 5, 1984.

Jacome, Augustine, August 23, 1984; August 30, 1984.

Jacome, Alex, Jr., February 13, 1984; June 7, 1984; April 25, 1985; July 22, 1985.

Jacome, Estela V. C. de, August 9, 1984; August 12, 1984.

Johnson, Peter, July 5, 1984.

Kaiserman, Flo, May 21, 1985.

Kaiserman, Nathan, May 21, 1985.

Kaiserman, Ken, May 21, 1985.

Levy, Leon, November 5, 1984.

Martinez, Toleta, August 7, 1984.

McMillan, Sam, June 20, 1984.

Middleton, Helen, July 29, 1985.

Olsen, Holden, August 7, 1984.

Peterson, Cele, August 21, 1984.

Quinto, Henry, January 11, 1984.

Sayre, Elina, October 2, 1984.

Valdez, Joel D., June 21, 1984.

LETTERS

DeConcini, Dennis to Alex G. Jacome, July 13, 1979. Jacome Papers, uncatalogued. Special Collections, The University of Arizona Library (hereafter cited as J.P.).

"Dick" of Society Brand Clothes to Alex Jacome, August 21, 1950. Jacome private papers in possession of Estela V. C. de Jacome.

Dillon, Edna to Alex G. Jacome, August 31, 1950 (J.P.).

Goldwater, Barry to The Honorable Robert Hill, August 21, 1957 (J.P.).

Goldwater, Barry to Alex Jacome, April 9, 1963 (J.P.).

Jacome, Alex G. to Lucille S. Abel, May 15, 1976 (J.P.).

Jacome, Alex G. to Mayor Lew Davis and City Councilmen, April 7, 1967 (J.P.).

Jacome, Alex G. to Lee Davis, August 2, 1965 (J.P.).

Jacome, Alex G. to Honorable Paul Fannin, March 17, 1970; May 7, 1975 (J.P.).

Jacome, Alex G. to Mr. John Burnham, August 14, 1957 (J.P.).

Jacome, Alex G. to Helen D. Seright, October 17, 1969 (J.P.).

Jacome, Alex G. to Ralph Nader, June 14, 1976 (J.P.).

Jacome, Alex G. to Senator Frank Felix, Douglas Holsclaw, and Carmen Cajero, November 21, 1973 (J.P.).

Jacome, Alex G. to Westbrook Pegler, September 5, 1957 (J.P.).

Jacome, Alex G. to Robert Fish, September 19, 1957 (J.P.).

Jacome, Alex G. to Mary Hamm Spencer, October 17, 1967 (J.P.).

Jacome, Alex G. to Senator Barry Goldwater, March 27, 1962 (J.P.).

Jacome Department Store to Dr. E. L. Larson, February 11, 1962 (J.P.).

Martinez, Gilbert to Alex G. Jacome, April 26, 1968 (J.P.).

Spencer, Mary Hamm to Jacome's Department Store, October 16, 1969 (J.P.).

Steele, D. H. to Alex G. Jacome, August 23, 1950 (J.P.).

Wilkey, Mrs. Frank D. to Alex G. Jacome, January 16, 1967 (J.P.).

NEWSPAPERS AND PERIODICALS

Arizona Daily Star (Tucson).

Arizona Highways.

Daily News Record (Tucson).

Department Store Journal.

El Sonorense (Hermosillo, Sonora, Mexico).

Newsweek.

Nogales Arizona International.

The Arizona Alumnus (Tucson).

The Los Angeles Examiner.

The Wall Street Journal.

Time.

Tucson Daily Citizen.

Tucsotarian.

Women's Wear Daily.

MANUSCRIPTS, DOCUMENTS, ARCHIVAL MATERIAL

"Alianza Hispano-Americana Observes Founder's Day Today."
    Clipping book, Arizona Heritage Center, Tucson,
    Arizona.

Book of Marriages, Pima County, May 18, 1891, p. 97, Carlos
    G. Jacome m. Dionisia Germán, filed June 3, 1891 by
    W. H. Calver, J.P.

Briegel, Kaye Lynn. "Alianza Hispano-Americana, 1894-
    1965." Unpublished doctoral dissertation in His-
    tory, University of Southern California, 1974.

Bufkin, Don. "The Broad Pattern of Land Use Change in
    Tucson, 1862-1912." *Territorial Tucson,* edited by
    Thomas F. Saarinen, manuscript in possession of Don
    Bufkin.

Chamber of Commerce. *Outlook.* Tucson, October 2, 1979, p.
    2.

Cosgrove, Richard. "Regionalism and Localism in Patterns
    of Mexican-American Discrimination: The Tucson
    Evidence." Unpublished paper in possession of
    Professor Cosgrove.

Devine, Mildred C. "An Evaluation of the Methods of Mer-
    chandise Control." Unpublished master's thesis in
    Education, The University of Arizona, 1959.

Emery, Fred. "A City in Action, 1951-1954: Four Years of
    Progress." Tucson: Office of the Mayor. In
    possession of Mrs. Emery, Tucson.

Figuero, Ramona, Sales slip, Jacome private papers in
    possession of Estela V. C. de Jacome, Tucson.

200

Goldstein, Marcy Gail. "Americanization and Mexicanization: The Mexican Elite and Anglo-Americans in the Gadsden Purchase Lands, 1853-1880." Unpublished doctoral dissertation, Department of History, Case Western University, 1977.

Harvill, Richard. Tucson. "Introduction to Mr. Alex G. Jacome to Newcomen Society, March 11, 1965." Jacome private papers in possession of Estela V. C. de Jacome, Tucson.

Index to Incorporations, Vol. 2, Pima County. Jacome's Department Store, Inc., Articles of Incorporation, January 26, 1928, Vol. 13, pp. 384-387.

Jacome Flyer. "Gilberto A. Jacome Memorial Day Special Opening for the Handicapped." December 4, 1978 (J.P.).

Jacome Department Store Christmas Card. December, 1959. In possession of Alex Jacome, Jr.

Jacome family photo album. In possession of Estela V. C. de Jacome.

Jacome, Alex G. "Address to the Tucson Women's Club," 1963 (J.P.).

"Jacome, Alex G." February 27, 1959. (J.P.).

La Paz, Bolivia trip clipping. Jacome private papers in possession of Estela V. C. de Jacome.

Levy, Leon. "Memoirs of Leon Levy." In possession of Levy family.

Marin, Eugene Acosta. "The Mexican-American Community and the Leadership of the Dominant Society." Unpublished doctoral dissertation in Anthropology, The University of Arizona, 1975.

"Newcomen Society Address" given by Alex G. Jacome. In possession of author, Professor Harwood Hinton.

Officer, James Eoff. "Sodalities and Systemic Linkage: The Joining Habits of Urban Mexican-Americans." Unpublished doctoral dissertation, Department of Anthropology, The University of Arizona, 1964.

Pettigrew, Andrew M. "The Creation of Organizational Cultures." Paper presented to the Joint ELIASM-Dansk Management Center Research Seminar on Entre-preneurs and the Process of Institution Building, Copenhagen (May 1976).

Spence, Allyn Gawain. "Variables Contributing to the Maintenance of the Mexican-American Societal Struc-ture in Tucson." Unpublished master's thesis in Anthropology, The University of Arizona, 1968, p. ix.

The Story of Jacomes Being the Story of the Life of Carlos Jacome Published on the Occassion [sic] of the 50th Anniversary of His Store. (March 1946) Tucson, Arizona (J.P.).

Tucson City Directory. 1881-1960.

Tucson Shopping Center Study: A Survey of Shopping Center Development and the Central Business District of Greater Tucson. Phoenix: Research and Development Department of the First National Bank, 1963, pp. 1-4.

Tucson Trade Bureau Analysis of Downtown. Los Angeles: Developmental Research Associates, 1969, p. 7.

BOOKS AND ARTICLES

Arellano, Richard. Strategies for Hispanic Business De-velopment: Trends and Implications. Washington, D.C.: National Chamber Foundation, 1984.

Strategies for Hispanic Business Development: Paths of Success, An Analysis of Case Studies. Washington, D.C.: National Chamber Foundation, 1984.

Strategies for Hispanic Business Development: Agenda for Action, Recommendations. Washington, D.C.: National Chamber Foundation, 1984.

Beals, Ralph. No Frontiers to Learning. Minneapolis: University of Minnesota Press, 1957.

Bernstein, Barton J. "The New Deal: The Conservative Achievements of Liberal Reform," Towards a New Past: Dissenting Essays in American History. New York: Pantheon Books, 1968, pp. 263-288.

Billington, Ray Allen (ed.). *The Frontier Thesis: Valid Interpretations of American History*. New York: Robert E. Kreege Publishing Co., 1977.

Bluestone, Barry; Hanna, Patricia; Kuhn, Sarah; and Moore, Laura. *The Retail Revolution, Market Transformation, Investment and Labor in the Modern Department Store*. Boston: Auburn House Publishing Co., 1984.

Brady, Maxine. *Bloomingdales*. New York: Harcourt, Brace, and Jovanovich, 1980.

Bret Harte, John. *Tucson: Portrait of a Desert Pueblo*. Woodland Hills, California: Windsor Publications, 1980, pp. 90, 138.

Cardosa, Lawrence A. *Mexican Emigration to the United States*. Tucson: The University of Arizona Press, 1980, p. 12.

Caywood, W. Eugene. *A History of Tucson Transportation*. Tucson: Pima County Historical Commission, n.d.

Chandler, Alfred D. *Strategy and Structure*. New York: Doubleday, 1962.

The Visible Hand: The Managerial Revolution in American Business. Cambridge, Massachusetts: The Belknap Press of Harvard University Press, 1977, pp. 438-450.

and Stephen Salsbury. *Pierre S. du Pont and the Making of the Modern Corporation*. New York: Harper and Row, 1971, pp. 49, 591-594, 644.

Clark, Thomas D. *Pills, Petticoats and Plows: The Country Store*. Norman: The University of Oklahoma Press, 1964.

Cochran, Thomas C. *The Puerto Rican Businessman*. Philadelphia: University of Pennsylvania Press, 1959.

Cohen, P. S. "Theories of Myth," *Man*, Vol. 4, 1969, pp. 337-353.

Commager, Henry Steele. *The American Mind: An Interpretation of American Thought and Character*. New Haven: Yale University Press, 1965, p. 18.

Dewey, John. *Democracy and Education*. New York: The Macmillan Co., 1916.

203

Dill, William R. "Environment as an Influence on Managerial Autonomy," *Administrative Science Quarterly*, Vol. 2, March 1978, pp. 409-443.

Divine, Robert. *American Immigration Policy, 1944-1952*. New Haven: Yale University Press, 1957, pp. 52-66.

Douglass, Elisha P. *The Coming of Age of American Business*. Chapel Hill: The University of North Carolina Press, 1971, p. 124.

Emmet, Boris and Jeuck, John E. *A History of Marshall Field and Co.* Philadelphia: University of Pennsylvania Press, 1976.

  A History of Sears, Roebuck and Company. Chicago: University of Chicago Press, 1950.

Ferry, John William. *A History of the Department Store*. New York: The Macmillan Company, 1960.

Getty, Harry T. *Interethnic Relationships in the Community of Tucson*. New York: Arno Press, 1976, pp. 113, 140-150, 195.

  Interethnic Relationships in the Community of Tucson. Doctoral dissertation, Microfilm, University of Chicago, 1950, pp. 238-240.

Gibbons, Herbert Adams. *John Wanamaker*. New York: Harper and Brothers, 1926.

Grebler, Leo; Moore, Joan; and Guzman, Ralph. *The Mexican-American People: The Nation's Second Largest Minority*. New York: The Free Press, 1970, pp. 66, 523-526, 535.

Harriman, Margaret Case. *And the Price is Right*. New York: The World Publishing Co., 1958.

Hendrickson, Robert. *The Grand Emporiums: The Illustrated History of America's Great Department Stores*. New York: Stein and Day, 1979.

Henry, John A. and Scavone, Cirino G. "Cars Stop Here," *Smoke Signal, Tucson Corral of the Westerners*, No. 23, Spring 1971.

Hewes, Gorden. "Mexicans in Search of 'The Mexican,'" *American Journal of Economics and Sociology*, Vol. 13, No. 2, January 1954, pp. 209-223.

Higham, John. *Strangers in the Land: Patterns of American Nativism, 1860-1925.* New York: Atheneum, 1963.

Hoffer, Eric. *The True Believer.* New York: Harper and Row, 1951, p. 45.

Hollon, Eugene. *The Southwest: Old and New.* New York: Alfred A. Knopf, 1961, p. 444.

Horn, Maurice (ed.). *The World Encyclopedia of Comics.* New York: Chelsea House, 1976, p. 145.

Jervey, William H., Jr. "When the Banks Closed," *Arizona and the West,* Vol. 10, Summer 1968, p. 143.

Juston, Neal. "Mexican-American Achievement Hindered by Cultural Conflict," *Sociology and Social Research,* July 1972, pp. 471-486.

Kanter, Rosabeth Moss. *Men and Women of the Corporation.* New York: Basic Books, Inc., 1977, pp. 119-120.

Kinzer, Donald. *An Episode in Anti-Catholicism: The American Protective Association.* Seattle: University of Washington Press, 1964.

Kirkland, Edward. *Dream and Thought in the Business Community, 1860-1900.* New York: Cornell University Press, 1956, pp. 13-20.

La Dame, Mary. *The Filene Store.* New York: n.p., 1930.

Lamar, Howard R. "Persistent Frontier: The West in the 20th Century," *Western Historical Quarterly,* January 1973, p. 15.

Luchsinger, L. Louise and Dunne, Patrick M. "Fair Trade Laws--How Fair?" *Journal of Marketing.* Worcester, Massachusetts: Hefferman Press, 1978, pp. 50-53.

Matthaei, Julie A. *An Economic History of Women in America: Women's Work, the Sexual Division of Labor and the Development of Capitalism.* New York: Schocken Books, 1982.

McWilliams, Carey. *North From Mexico: The Spanish-Speaking People in the United States.* New York: Greenwood Press, 1968.

Miles, Robert H. *Macro Organizational Behavior.* Santa Monica, California: Goodyear Publishing, Inc., 1980, p. 190.

Millan, Verna Carleton. *Mexico Reborn*. Boston: Houghton Mifflin Co., 1939, p. 15.

Miller, Michael V. "Variations in Mexican-American Family Life: A Review Synthesis of Empirical Research," *Aztlan*, Vol. 9, Fall 1978, pp. 209-231.

Mills, C. Wright. *The Power Elite*. New York: Oxford University Press, 1956, pp. 12, 36-39, 43.

   White Collar: The American Middle Class. New York: Oxford University Press, 1953, pp. 36, 50, 57, 164, 1973.

Moore, Joan. *Mexican-Americans*. Englewood Cliffs, New Jersey: Prentice-Hall, Inc., 1970, p. 11.

Morgan, Howard E. "The Changing Structure of the Distributive Trades in Arizona," Part II, *Arizona Review*, Vol. 9, No. 3, March 1960, pp. 1-23.

Nichols, Dale. *The Story of Carlos Jacome*. Tucson: The Pioneer Press, 1955.

Officer, James Eoff. "Historical Factors in Interethnic Relations in the Community of Tucson," *Arizoniana*, Fall 1960, pp. 12-16.

Pace, Ann. "Mexican Refugees in Arizona, 1910-1911," *Arizona and the West*, Spring 1974, pp. 5-18.

Pasdermadjian, Grant. *The Department Store: Its Origins, Evolution, and Economics*. New York: Arno Press, 1976.

Pfeffer, Jeffrey and Salancik, Gerald R. *The External Control of Organizations: A Resource Dependence Perspective*. New York: Harper and Row, 1976, p. 190.

Pilat, Oliver. *Pegler: Angry Man of the Press*. Boston: Beacon Press, 1963, pp. 100-111, 151, 188.

Porter, Glenn. *The Rise of Big Business, 1860-1910*. Northbrook, Illinois: AHM Publishing Corporation, 1973.

Potter, David M. *People of Plenty: Economic Abundance and the American Character*. Chicago: The University of Chicago Press, 1954.

Raaf, Daniel W. "Downtown Tucson and the Woman Shopper,"
    Arizona Business and Economic Review, Vol. 7, No.
    4, April 1958, p. 8.

Ramos, Samuel. *Profile of Man and Culture in Mexico*,
    translated by Peter G. Earle. Austin: University
    of Texas Press, 1962, p. 26.

*Recent Economic Trends in the United States: Report of the
    President's Research Committee on Recent Economic
    Changes of the President's Conference on Unemploy-
    ment*, Vol. III. New York: McGraw-Hill, 1929, p.
    666.

*Recent Social Trends in the United States: Report of the
    President's Research Committee on Social Trends*.
    New York: McGraw-Hill, 1933, p. 867.

Romanell, Patrick. *Making of the Mexican Mind*. South
    Bend, Indiana: University of Notre Dame Press,
    1967.

Romo, Ricardo and Paredes, Raymund (eds.). *New Directions
    in Chicano Scholarship*. San Diego: University of
    California, San Diego, 1978.

Ryan, Franklin W. "Family Finance in the United States,"
    Journal of Business of the University of Chicago,
    October 1930, p. 417.

Schumpeter, Joseph. *Capitalism, Socialism, and Democracy*,
    3rd edition. New York: Harper and Row, 1942, pp.
    81-86, 131-142.

Scott, William G. *Organizational Theory: A Structure and
    Behavioral Analysis*. Homewood, Illinois: Richard
    D. Irwin, Inc., 1983, p. 333.

Sonnichsen, C. L. *Tucson: The Life and Times of an Ameri-
    can City*. Norman: The University of Oklahoma
    Press, 1982.

Steele, Fred I. *Physical Settings and Organizational
    Development*. Reading, Massachusetts: Addison-
    Wesley, 1973, p. 38.

Stinchcombe, Arthur. "Social Structure and Organizations,"
    in *Handbook of Organizations*, James G. March (ed.).
    Chicago: Rand-McNally, 1965, pp. 142-193.

Sturdivant, Frederick D. *Business and Society: A Managerial Approach.* Homewood, Illinois: Richard D. Irwin, Inc., 1981, p. 27.

Thompson, James. *Organizations in Action.* New York: McGraw-Hill, 1967, pp. 27-28.

Twyman, Robert W. *History of Marshall Field and Company.* Philadelphia: University of Pennsylvania Press, 1976.

Tyler, E. B. *Primitive Culture,* 3rd English edition. London: John Murray Publishers, Ltd., 1891.

Vatter, Harold G. *The U.S. Economy in the 1950's: An Economic History.* New York: W. W. Norton and Co., 1963, pp. 93-94, 116.

Walker, Bruce J. "Arizona Retailers on Fair Trade Repeal," *Arizona Business,* Vol. XXIII. Phoenix: Bureau of Business and Economic Research, Arizona State University, 1975, pp. 20-28.

Weber, David (ed.). *Foreigners in Their Native Land.* Albuquerque: University of New Mexico Press, 1973.

Worth, James C. *Shaping an American Institution.* Urbana: University of Illinois Press, 1984, p. 26.

Zorn, Burton A. and Felman, George J. *Business Under the New Price Laws: A Study of the Economic and Legal Problems Arising Out of the Robinson-Patman Act and the Various Fair Trade and Unfair Practices Laws.* New York: Prentice Hall, 1937, Vol. XI, pp. 126-127.